Orthographs

The Stavros Niarchos Foundation Cultural Center

Orthographs

The Stavros Niarchos Foundation Cultural Center

Photographs by

Yiorgis Yerolymbos

Introduction by Renzo Piano
Essays by Katharine Storr and Robert Storr, and Yiorgis Yerolymbos

Distributed by Yale University Press, New Haven and London

Foreword

In the era of Instagram, Snapchat, and selfies, is it possible for photographs to build a comprehensive narrative? As John Berger writes in his 1972 essay "Understanding a Photograph":

> A photograph is a result of the photographer's decision that it is worth recording that this particular event or this particular object has been seen. If everything that existed were continually being photographed, every photograph would become meaningless. A photograph celebrates neither the event itself nor the faculty of sight in itself. A photograph is already a message about the event it records. The urgency of the message is not entirely dependent on the urgency of the event, but neither can it be entirely independent from it. At its simplest, the message, decoded, means: *I have decided that seeing this is worth recording.*

At a time when the incessant use of smartphones to photograph everything around us, including ourselves, is perhaps (as Berger suggests) rendering photographs "meaningless"—or at least less meaningful—Yiorgis Yerolymbos's meticulous and thorough visual documentation of the construction of the Stavros Niarchos Foundation Cultural Center (SNFCC) points in a different direction, recalling and restoring photography's storytelling ability.

In this body of work, which was created over a span of nine years and in thousands of photographs, Yerolymbos not only recounts the story of the realization of Renzo Piano's design, he also captures a seminal moment in the ongoing transformation of the city's urban landscape.

The SNFCC is destined to become an Athenian landmark. But the very notion of *landmark* requires a time-based understanding of a particular *topos* and landscape—that is to say, an understanding of a *before* and an *after*. Yerolymbos's photographs reveal in detail what the site looked like before the start of construction and how it has gradually changed to become what it is today, at the completion of the building; in this way he offers a visual map as well as an investigation into the emergence of a landmark.

Construction sites are complex, dynamic, active, crowded, ever-changing environments. Their interaction with the natural landscape is often intensely physical,

sometimes even violent. They involve large numbers of people from a range of backgrounds, with different skills and playing a variety of roles; they involve raw materials and working equipment, from the most basic to the most technologically advanced. To the unfamiliar eye, a construction site may look anarchic; the proposition to construct a narrative coherence out of it may seem a dauntingly complicated task.

Each of Yerolymbos's photographs captures and preserves an isolated moment in the life of the construction site of the SNFCC. Viewed individually, the photographs are formally striking, but their meaning is somewhat inscrutable, since the viewer (unlike the photographer) has no sense of their specific spatial or temporal contexts. The meaning of these images is inextricably linked with photographer's decision to record particular moments, and his attempt to connect those unique moments into a coherent narrative of *before* and *after*.

The larger meaning of the project becomes clearer upon considering the full agglomeration of these pictures. In entrusting Yerolymbos with the task of creating a visual documentation of this construction project, we put our faith in his ability to select from thousands of unique moments a sequence of images that, viewed together, carry the ability to tell the story of how an extraordinary project came into existence.

This volume is an invitation to join Yerolymbos on a personal journey into the heart of this remarkable construction: its beginning, its middle, and its end. It is also an attempt to give some sense of permanence to a process that is by definition ever-changing. We are deeply grateful to Yiorgis Yerolymbos for inviting us on this voyage, and for telling this story.

Andreas Dracopoulos
Co-President
Stavros Niarchos Foundation

Introduction

RENZO PIANO

There is nothing more beautiful than a construction site. To a photographer, it's a marvel. To me, it's my life.

I am the son of a builder. My father had a small construction company in Genoa, where I was born. He built small things, but the magic of seeing a building grow day by day to completion is unique, and it does not depend on the building's dimensions. I spent my childhood watching as the pieces that make up a building were brought together—as in a game—and became a wall, a roof, a house.

One day, as a boy, I told my father I wanted to be an architect. He looked at me and asked: "Why become an architect if you can be a builder? It's here on the building site that things get made." It was as though I was betraying his vision of building, and basically he was right.

Perhaps because of this, I consider myself a craftsman—a *builder* rather than an architect—in short, someone who puts together the pieces that then become a building. For this reason, my office is called the Building Workshop.

This book tells a story in photographs of the most beautiful adventure of a building: the construction site. It is a wondrous place, made up of elements that move, suspended objects that mingle and intersect without ever touching, and day by day they are transformed, they are combined, and sometimes they disappear. A construction site is a constantly changing landscape. The many pieces that comprise it move continuously, with unimaginable lightness.

All this brings back another part of my childhood: the weekends when my father took me to visit the Port of Genoa. A port, by definition, is a permanent construction site. Everything floats on the water or in the air, defying gravity, even though tons and tons of material are being moved. The cranes have the starring role. They are magical, juggling things, moving things about and putting them together as if by enchantment, in a dance that continuously redesigns the landscape.

On a construction site like that of the Stavros Niarchos Foundation Cultural Center (SNFCC), large and complex, there were so many cranes—more than ten—that the ballet among them was incredible.

So in the summer of 2014 we decided to make them *really* dance.

And for an evening, accompanied by the Greek National Opera Orchestra, the cranes on the construction site of the SNFCC danced in time to the music. It was a little craze, or game if you prefer, that could be possible only when the building site is huge and there are lots of cranes.

A construction site is made up of working people, and it is often multicultural and multiethnic. Different nationalities come together and have to work together. The cultures are mixed, the languages mingle in a sort of Babel, and we sometimes wonder how we can ever arrive at the final result. But still the magic of the building site makes things happen, cultures come together, and miraculously everything takes shape.

The photographs in this book capture the magic of the place, the marvel of continuous change and growth. Thousands of shots, taken day after day, tell this remarkable story in pictures.

An Acropolis for Our Time

KATHARINE STORR AND ROBERT STORR

Great public projects are not necessarily the fruit of great prosperity. Often they have been quite the opposite. Sometimes the need to kick-start a stalled economy and raise employment through government investment has prompted them. On other occasions public projects have been initiated by governments with the aim of restoring confidence in a beleaguered and demoralized society. In yet other cases, most frequently in the arts, they have resulted from the eagerness of private interests to contribute to the cultural commonwealth. Never before to our knowledge have the first two aims been so fully realized under the aegis of the third.

That is to say, it is virtually impossible to think of another instance in the modern era in which a private foundation that is devoted to enhancing culture in all its dimensions, to the sciences and humane approaches to them, and to better understanding among diverse social groups, finds itself in the position of providing an entire nation—and for that matter a struggling continent in an embattled world— with a wholly positive example of what can be achieved when people of different backgrounds and perspectives put their minds to a collective good. Especially not in a context where many of their fellow citizens have given up hope for shared improvements in their lives and resigned themselves to perpetual setbacks and incremental losses rather than actual gains. Yet all this is precisely true of the Stavros Niarchos Foundation Cultural Center (SNFCC).

Given its magnitude and urban majesty, one might be tempted to use the adjective "pharaonic" for the project in question. But we are but in Greece, not in Egypt, and we are speaking of something built for the betterment of the *polis*, not to glorify a ruler or personification of the State. Moreover, we are not concerned with something built in ancient times by armies of slaves, but rather a magnificent structure erected by architects, engineers, and skilled labor in a twenty-first-century democracy. Indeed, in his introduction to this book devoted to the SNFCC, Renzo Piano, its principal designer, makes eloquently plain that his perspective on the conception and realization of this massive undertaking is that of a builder. He is a builder whose vocation implicitly encompasses the concerns of all those engaged in bringing into being this complex, multipurpose ensemble of the Greek National Opera, the National Library of Greece, and a huge public garden.

How can one document the cumulative growth of such an organism? How can one possibly do so considering its many components? Its natural setting, as well as its

many constructed tiers and facets? For given the SNFCC's emphasis on assuring that the Center is maintained by ecologically responsible support systems, and its preoccupation with the Center's integration into the existing fabric of a zone between two cities that has taken form and knitted together over generations—on the one hand, greater Athens, and on the other, the Port of Piraeus—we are thus speaking about a place and a period of history at which organic metaphors are more essential to grasping the possibilities for present and future urbanization than were any of the utopian, quasi-science-fictional models for the total transformation, if not total domination or colonization, of the habitable (or sometimes virtually uninhabitable) environment in so much of twentieth-century discourse about architecture and city planning.

So, following the lead of Yiorgis Yerolymbos, the photographer charged with this theoretically and practically daunting challenge, let us begin to answer our own question by drawing attention first to the temporal rather than spatial dimensions of the problem. As everyone knows, Rome was not built in a day, and neither, of course, was Athens, ancient or modern. However, contemporary construction— and in many burgeoning metropolises the precipitous demolition of very recent buildings and their rapid replacement by the next generation of "the new" occurs at a dizzyingly rapid pace—entails preparation of the terrain, gathering of materials, thoughtful division and delegation of labor, the painstaking parceled-out fabrication of elements unique to the architect's conception, and so much more.

As to custom fabrication, there are many examples in Piano's design for the SNFCC. Among them are the solar panels, individually tailored by technicians and workers, in a parking lot adjacent to the long reflecting pool that serves as the dominant axis for the Center's layout. They were fabricated even as work was in progress on the monumental theater and the crowning pavilion these panels would cap, and for which they would provide clean energy. Roughly assembled from rebar and cement, thinly trowelled to the finest tolerances, the panels were then clad with light-sensitive coverings, and these individually crafted "sandwiches" are destined for the roof of the "lantern" set atop the layered spaces of the National Opera house, which, like the National Library, is located below grade in the park surrounding the SNFCC. The genius of Piano's scheme consists largely of having effectively concealed "underground"—that is, under an artificial terrace of vast proportions— a gargantuan amalgam of highly specialized purpose-designed structures with multiple entrances that would have been overbearing and accessible from only one level had they risen from that terrace like a conventional urban tower or architectural block.

When at long last such pieces—and there are many more of them—are ready and begin to fall into place, the rate of visible change at the site accelerates dramatically, before slowing down again while interior finishes and technical elements are completed by other crews of workmen. Imagine an anthill swarming with highly skilled ants, ants that are fully conscious of the importance of what they are doing and deeply invested in it. Ants that are not insects at all; they are sentient beings who would be dwarfed by the scale of the "anthill" they are making, were it not for the fact that the architect has taken special care to ensure that each and every aspect of the site, as seen from each and every vantage point, retains an affirmative human scale. He has done so out of respect for the people who will give substance

to his grand vision, as well as those who will use it, whether as performers or members of the general public, as scholars and librarians gathering and protecting the written word, or simply as casual readers savoring the wealth of texts made available to them, or, for that matter, as pedestrians out for a stroll.

The authors of this essay were able to view the SNFCC *in medias res*, initially in the winter of 2014 and again, near its completion, in the spring of 2016. Photographer Yiorgis Yerolymbos, however, has had it in his sights for the duration of its construction. Ingeniously, he solved the problem of recording the Center's gradual emergence by selecting a singular vantage point high above it, viewing it as do flying birds, or more precisely as do swinging cranes (mechanical rather than avian cranes, that is). To reach such heights, Yerolymbos was obliged to schedule one of these elegant icons of modern engineering during off-hours so that it could take him up as far as practically possible, where, with the exceptional mobility of these slender mini-skyscrapers, he could study the activity below. Of the finite number of these gigantic pieces of equipment available anywhere in the world at any given time, there were eleven stationed at the SNFCC, indicating the magnitude of the undertaking. From the top of one or another of them, Yerolymbos was thus in a position to survey all quadrants of the site. And, rather than gazing at wide vistas visible from his perch, he looked straight down using the frame of his lens to grid out the space beneath him as his shutter froze the movement of men and machines.

Accordingly, his images amount to stop-action vignettes of the ongoing stratification and structural articulation of an immense edifice. In Yerolymbos's own way of thinking, the pertinent aesthetic references encompass the Düsseldorf School of photographers trained by Bernd and Hilla Becher, and the New Topographics photographers of the built environment in North America, such as Lewis Baltz, Joe Deal, and Robert Adams, as well as photographer, painter, and graphic artist Ed Ruscha, master of the deadpan look at the urban vernacular. But they also include the experimental pioneer of arrested moving pictures Eadweard Muybridge, except that Muybridge's sequential documentation of animals and humans in motion were shot against a matrix mounted vertically behind his subjects—in architectural terminology this view is called an "elevation"—whereas Yerolymbos's photographs are more akin to an architectural plan, or chart. However, as noted before, the grids with which he works are not of his creation, but rather, thanks to Piano's design, inherent in the structures he examines. As such, to borrow from the Dada vocabulary of Marcel Duchamp, they are "readymades."

Nevertheless, the strong shadows cast on the ground by the Mediterranean sun (page 101) turn that plane into a foil for the movement of everyone and everything onsite. And so a helmeted man striding across a freshly poured tectonic plate appears in *plan*, as a stationary form, while his shadow stretches in *elevation*— albeit horizontally—across the cured concrete floor. Such optical paradoxes would no doubt have amused Duchamp.

Yet if Duchamp, the inventor of the readymade, was the ostensible enemy of what he called "retinal art"—by which he meant painting, even though he was a well-known and much-consulted connoisseur of the medium—the most pronounced aesthetic parallels suggested by Yerolymbos's pictures of the SNFCC are paintings of the postwar era, from Art Informel and gestural abstraction of the 1940s

Franz Kline
Untitled, 1947
Brush and black ink on wove paper
43.3 × 67 cm

Pierre Soulages
Peinture (*Painting*), 1957
Oil on canvas
194.8 × 129.8 cm

Alberto Burri
Grande Cretto Nero (*Big Black Crack*)
Mixed media
149.5 × 249.5 cm

Giuseppe Uncini
Cementarmato (*Reinforced Concrete*), 1961
Concrete and steel
99 × 198 cm

Robert Morris
Untitled (*Pink Felt*), 1970
Felt pieces of various sizes
Overall dimensions variable

and 1950s to Minimalism, Hard Edge, and Arte Povera of the 1960s and 1970s. Consider the dominant compositional element of the photograph just cited: a wide swath of black immediately to the right of the walking worker. Presumably tar or some kind of waterproofing sealant, the material amounts to an abstract emblem, which, as indicated by textures picked up by Yerolymbos's camera, was brushed or broomed on, in such a way that it resembles a huge work by Franz Kline, Piero Manzoni, or Pierre Soulages (pages 101, 133, and 29).

In other photographs, the rebar and forms for pouring concrete result in an intricate geometric composition of variable modules that is worthy of the Lithuanian painter Kestutis Zapkus (pages 124 and 125).

Moreover, it is impossible not to see in yet other photographs (pages 69 and 105 for example) direct correspondences to the Italians Alberto Burri and Giuseppe Uncini, or the early monochromes of the German Zero artists Günther Uecker and Otto Piene.

This is not to say that such referents are in any sense to be taken as conscious inspirations for Yerolymbos's artistry. Instead, the point being made is that, in their complexity and rigor, these photographs far exceed the demands of reportage. They are much more than an exercise in taking account of the details of erecting a building, although they certainly accomplish that goal. Indeed, they are so rich in telling details—what Roland Barthes called *puncta* in the overall photographic field—as to seem inexhaustibly interesting at that level, meaning no offense at the "Where's Waldo?" level of photographic scrutiny. From that perspective, the workmen and their sun-cast doppelgängers are all Waldos, as is, in its way, the shadow of the crane from which Yerolymbos observes them, making the artist himself an *über*-Waldo of sorts.

Look down. What else does one see through his lens?

Oh, so many things. Two of Yerolymbos's shots feature the green tufted grid of plantings in the garden laid out by Piano's collaborator, landscape-architect Deborah Nevins (pages 80 and 99). Her notion was that the environs of the Center should mirror the indigenous flora of the region, both out of consideration for what is distinctive about it and to ensure that such a garden would not become an alien "ornamental" feature that was unnecessarily costly to maintain.

Accordingly, the coloration of the trees and shrubs against the reddish earth is relatively muted, as it is in many parts of the Mediterranean Basin, even as those trees are rich in shapes and textures. When the garden comes to maturity, its intrinsic characteristics will become more pronounced; while it may seem spare in these pictures, as glimpses of its present state they also presage its eventual fruition in tantalizing ways. This green space is like the sketch an artist makes on bare canvas before filling in and fully tinting the forms. Be that as it may, nothing can compete with the intensity of modern artificial pigments, and Yerolymbos relishes such contrasts. Thus another photograph, taken closer to the ground, centers on a cluster of bright, acid-blue-green lozenges dumped on the russet terrain like so many pick-up-sticks on a game board, French fries on a plate, or modules in a contemporary sculptural "scatter piece" (page 85).

From the photographer's vantage point, Nevins's garden is well-apportioned and chromatically subtle, while the construction site is, by comparison, jumbled and garish. Nature harnessed by culture is juxtaposed with man-made things on the verge of chaos.

Overall, one might say that the inherent drama of Yerolymbos's pictures, a drama visible on the surface of his imagery but also palpable beneath the surface of everything he shows us, is the drama of order and disorder playing itself out over months and years, layer upon layer of a rising monument we see in each photograph as a ground plane pressurized from beneath. In the same way, the most "natural" of these views are in reality pictures of an alternately dusty and verdant garden, built over a maze of subterranean chambers that encases the SNFCC like the shell over the endoskeleton of a crab. As to the drama of order and disorder, the leeway for confusion on a construction site is nil, the consequences of accidents being catastrophic. So what may seem to be the casual dispersion of materials, tools, and bodies, held up for our inspection by Yerolymbos's artistry, is in reality the meticulous choreography of the myriad constituents of the builder's trade—which, like modern dance itself, tolerates a preordained degree of improvisation.

Piano himself understands this, as evidenced by the "ballet" of construction cranes he staged in the summer of 2014. Presently these machines are completing their tasks and will soon move on to other jobs, as will the teams of men and women who have devoted so much of their time, energy, and creative intelligence to this heroic effort. Soon the swarms of people responsible for shaping this extraordinary place—this new Acropolis—will be replaced by the swarms of those who will use and enjoy it. They will be followed in turn by generations more to come. All the while, Yerolymbos's photographs will remain as a permanent archive of images of the ever-changing configuration of forces that resulted in the Stavros Niarchos Foundation Cultural Center, as an homage paid by one artist, the photographer, and one art form, photography, to another: Renzo Piano, along with his team of architects and the craftsmen who realized their designs. This building will henceforth be a fixture on the horizon of one of the world's oldest cities as well as a wager on its long-term future. These pictures will endure as a testament to the solicitude that this designer and this patron had for the holistic approach to their ambitious intervention, and to collective optimism.

Plates

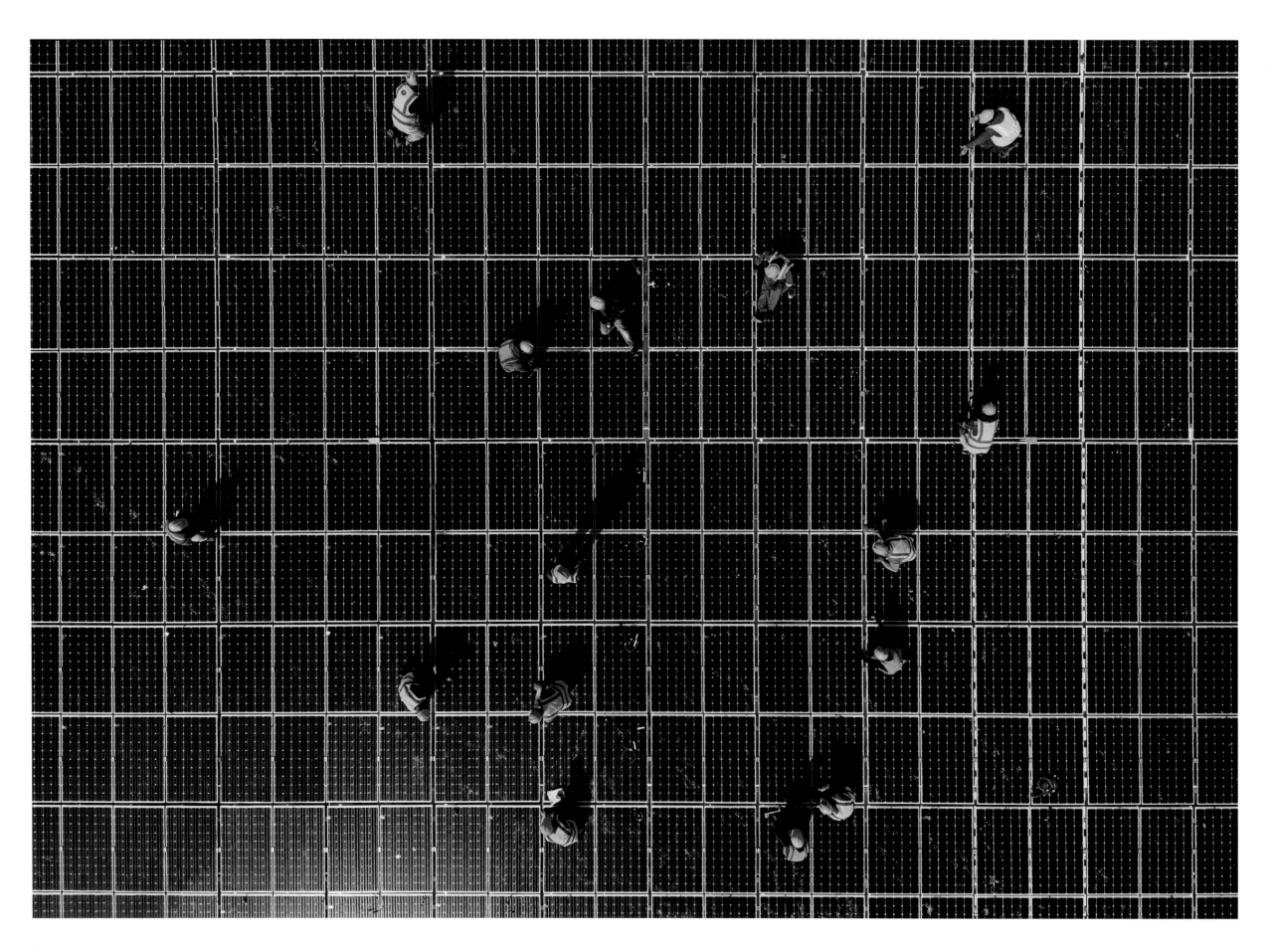

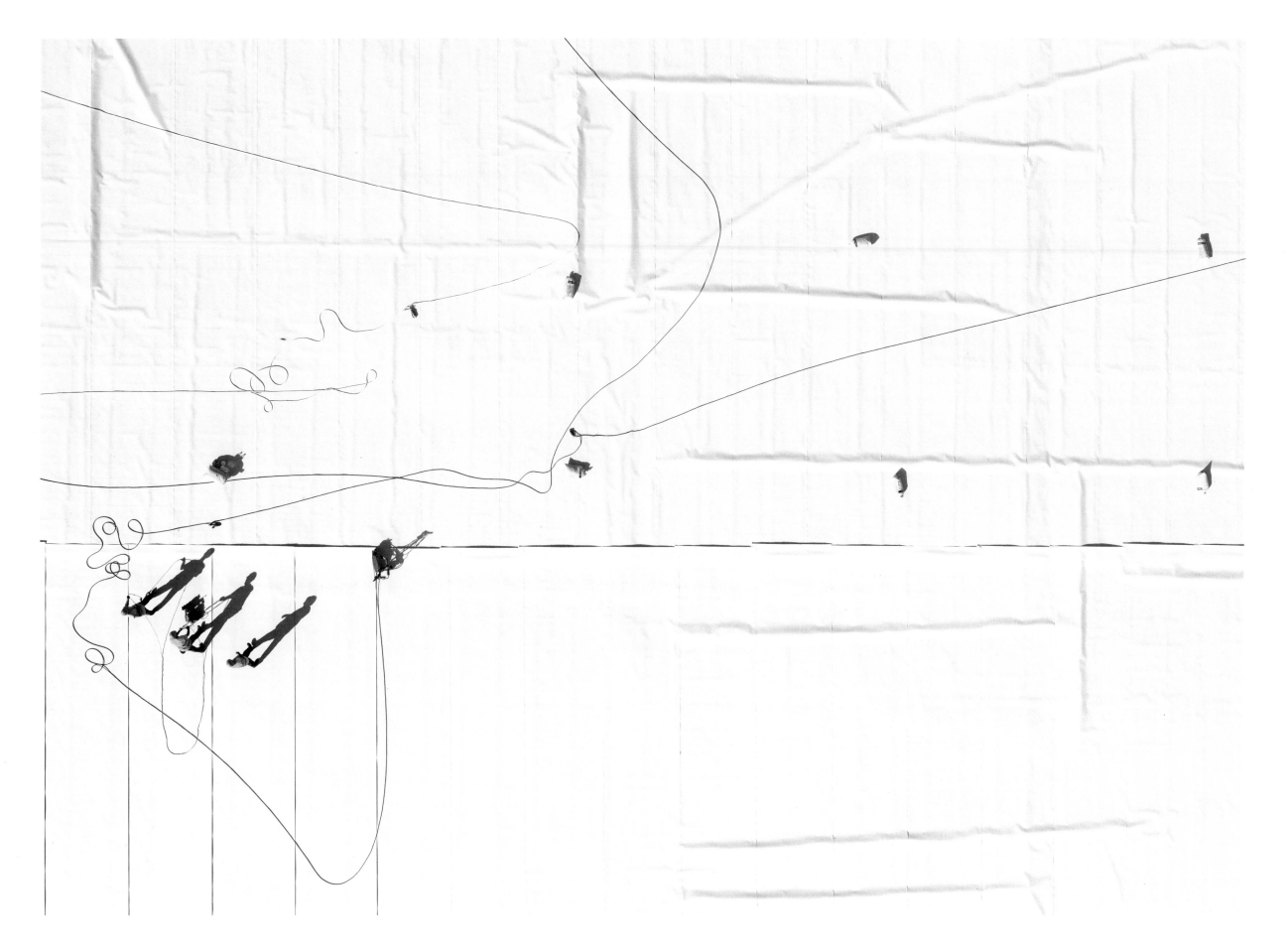

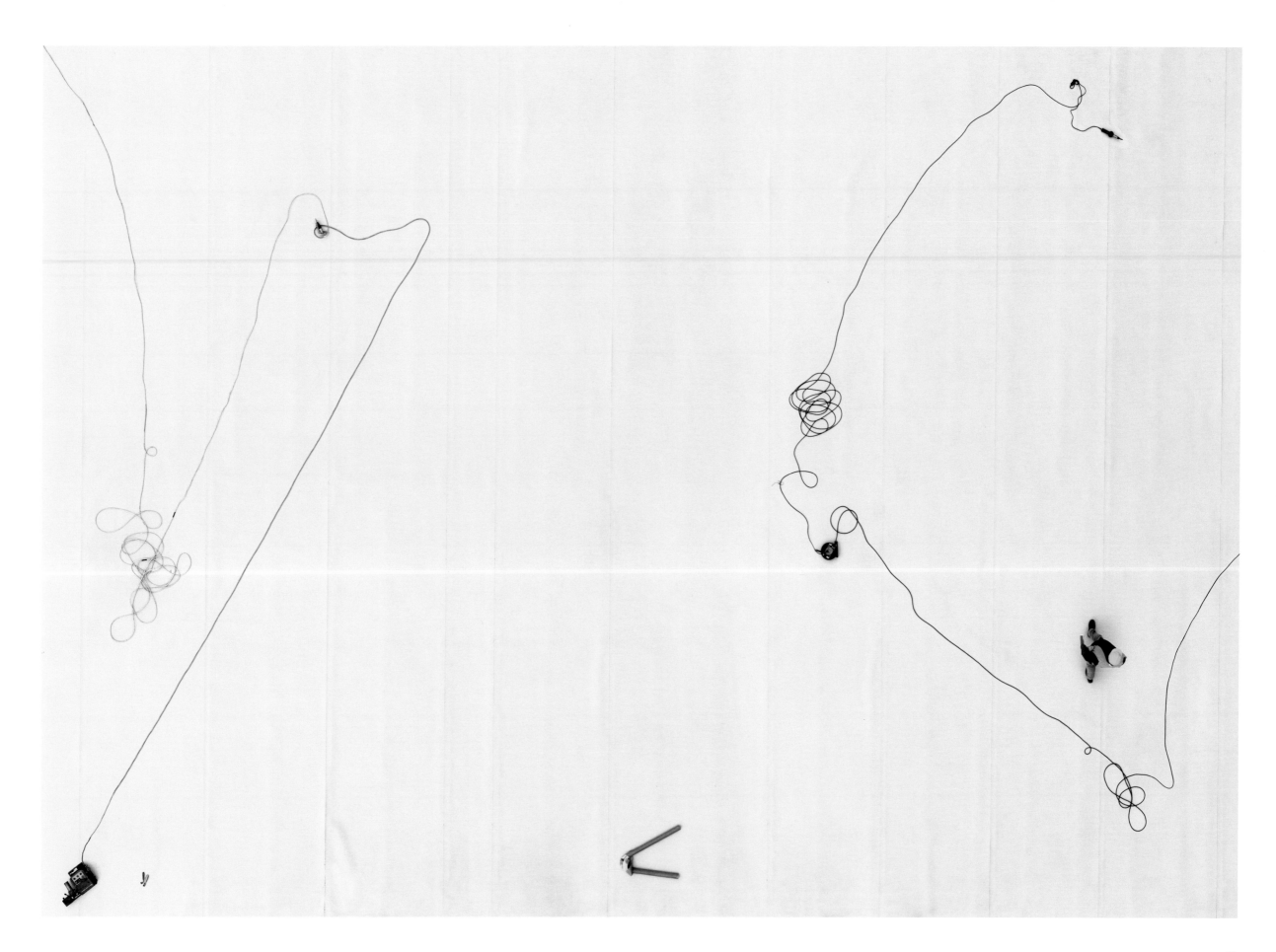

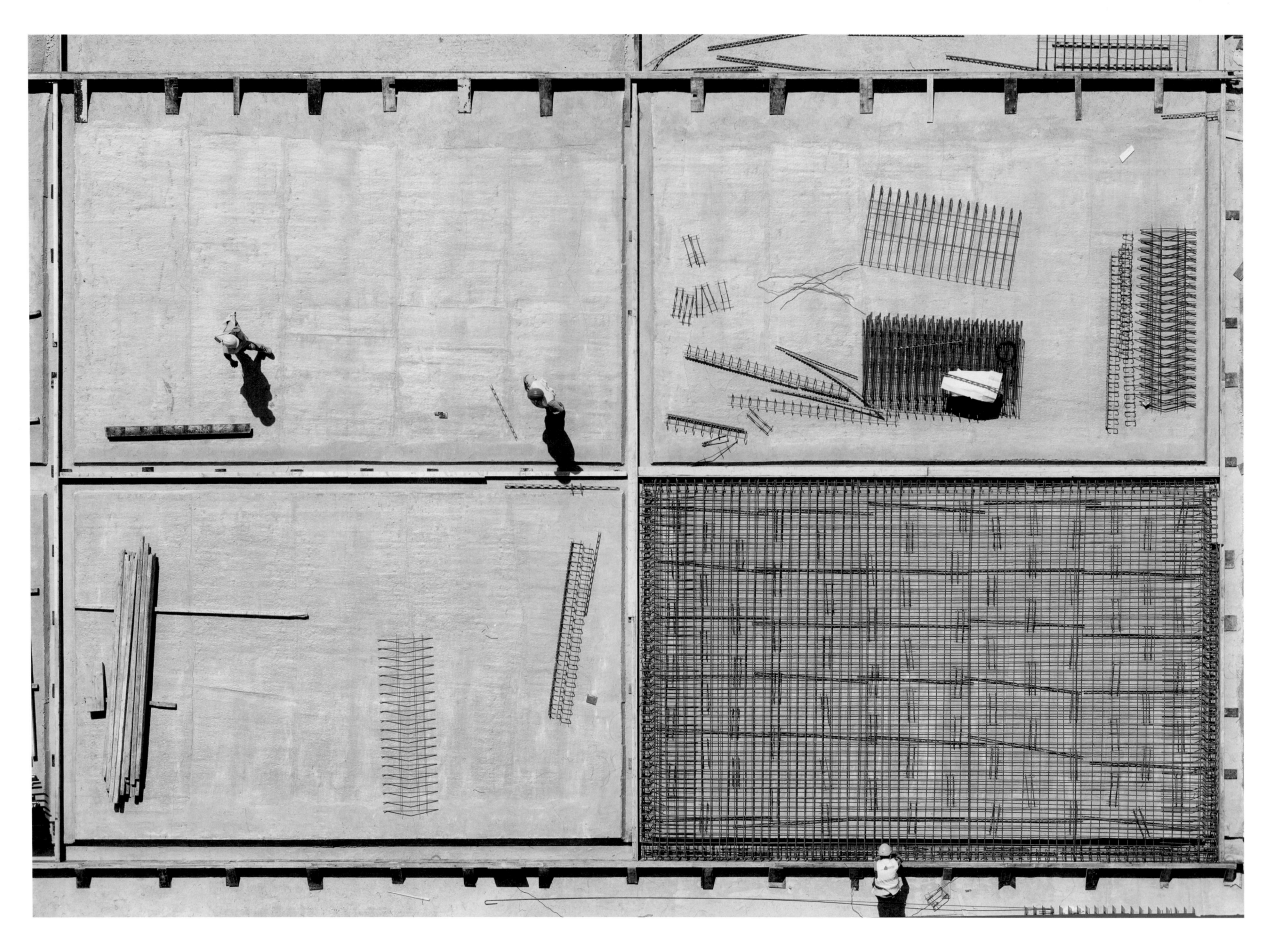

41

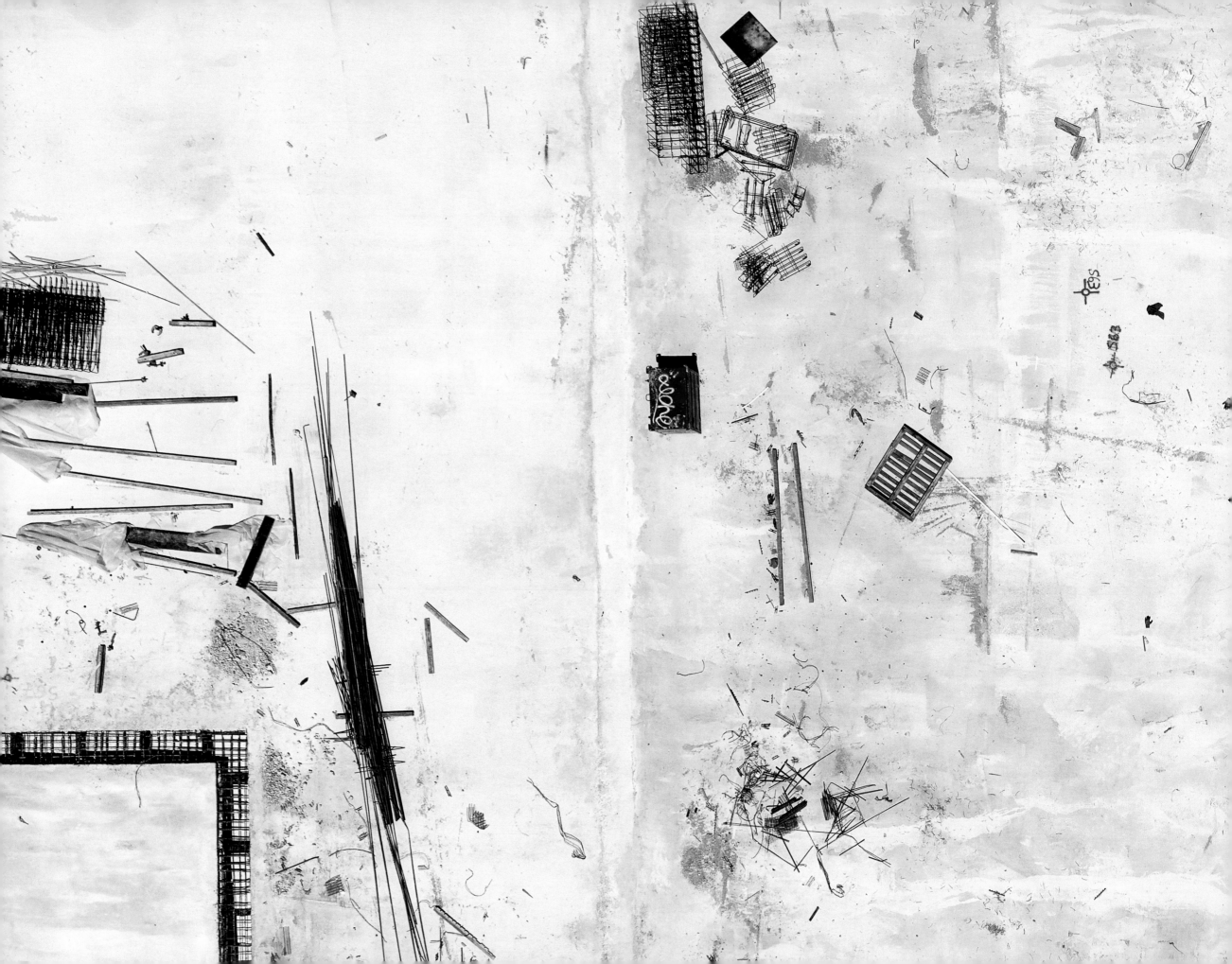

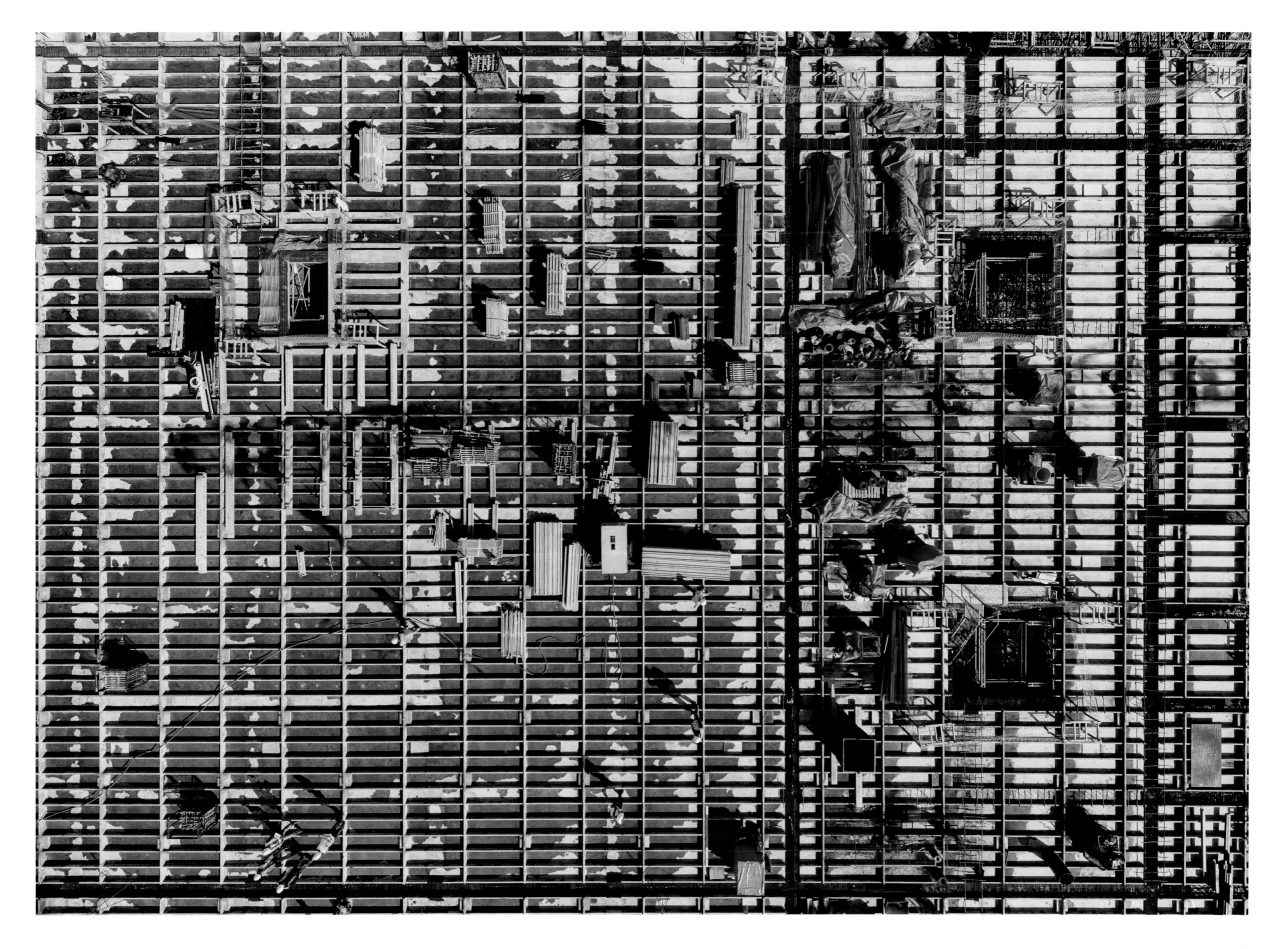

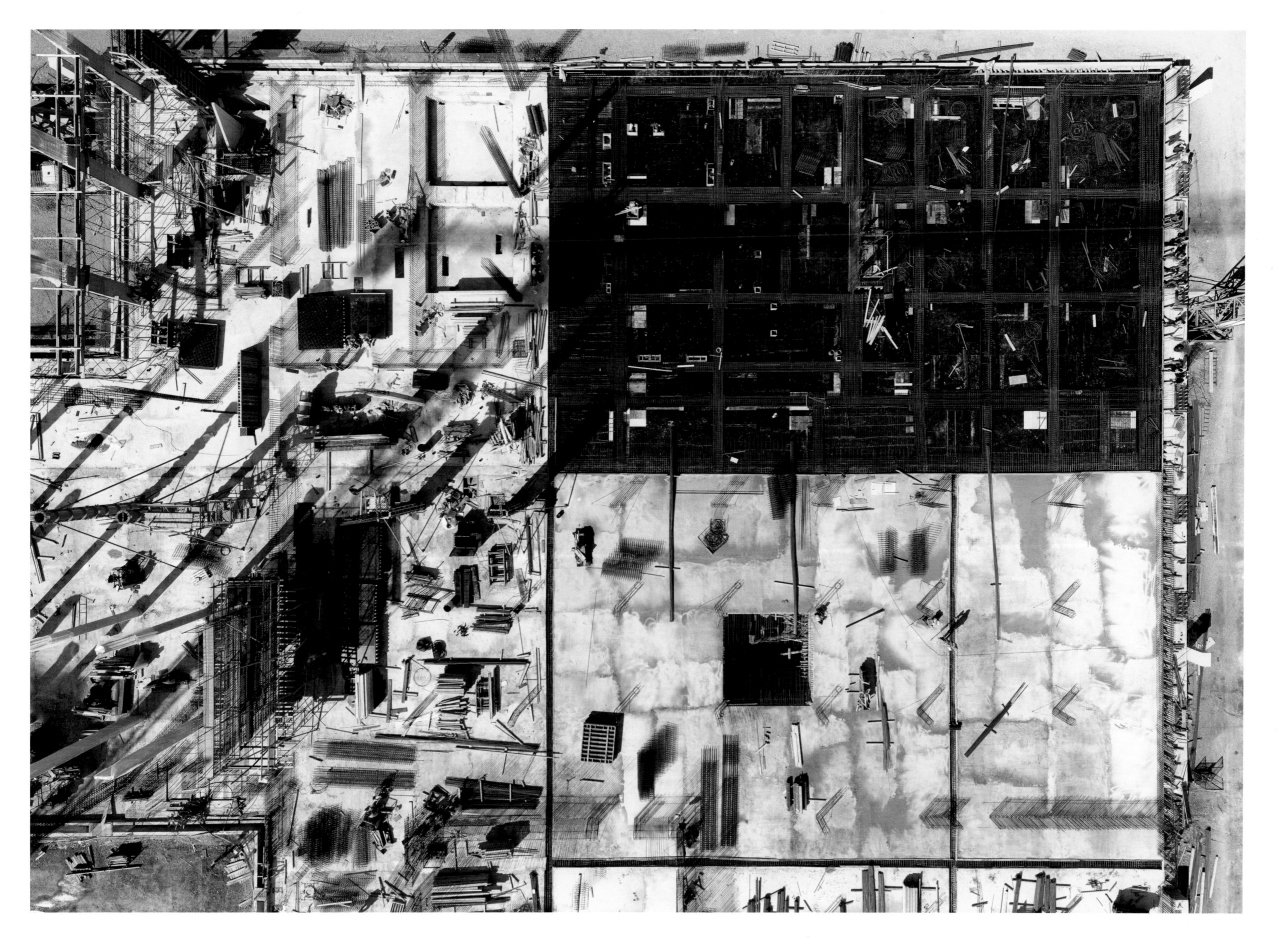

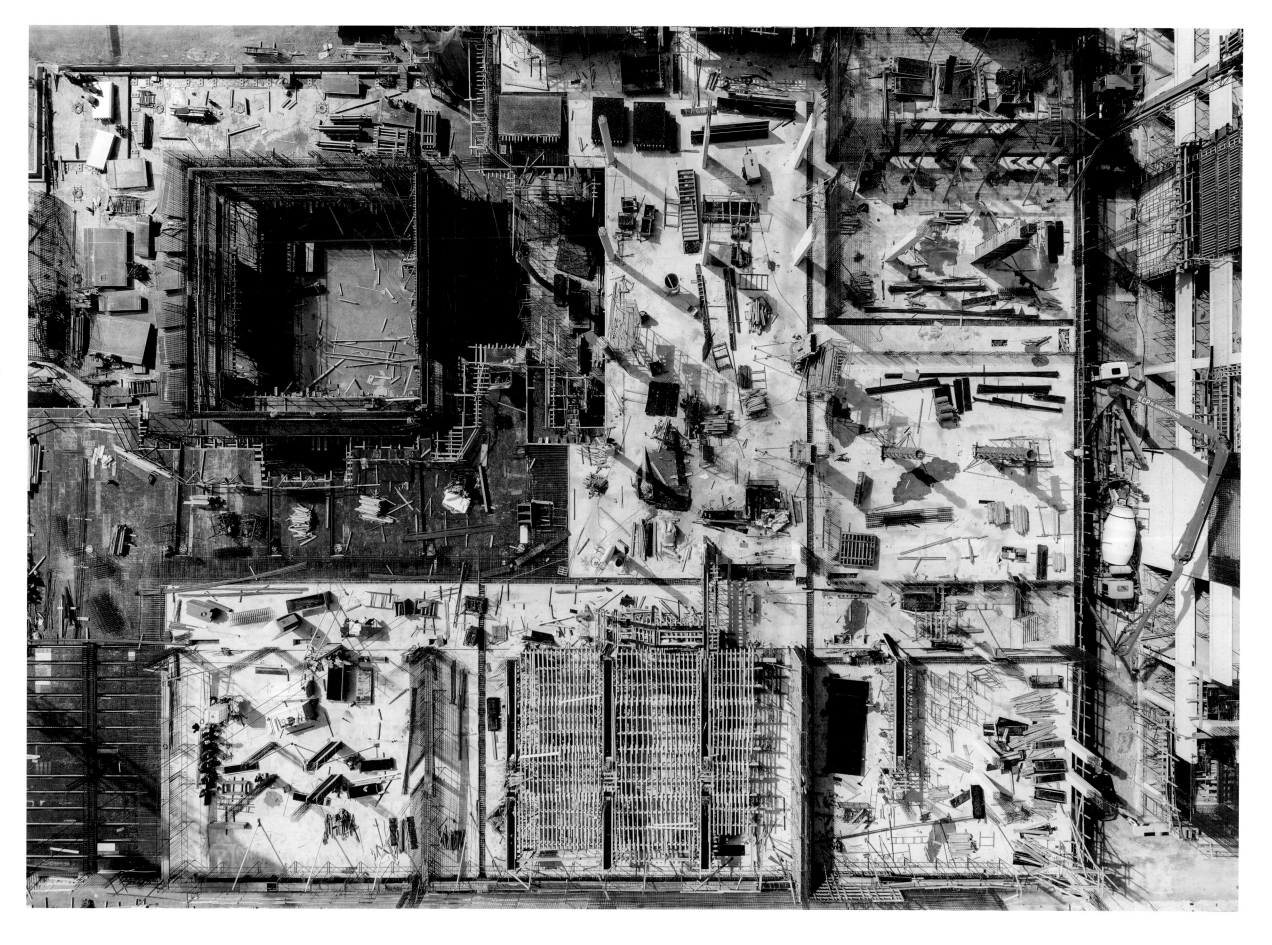

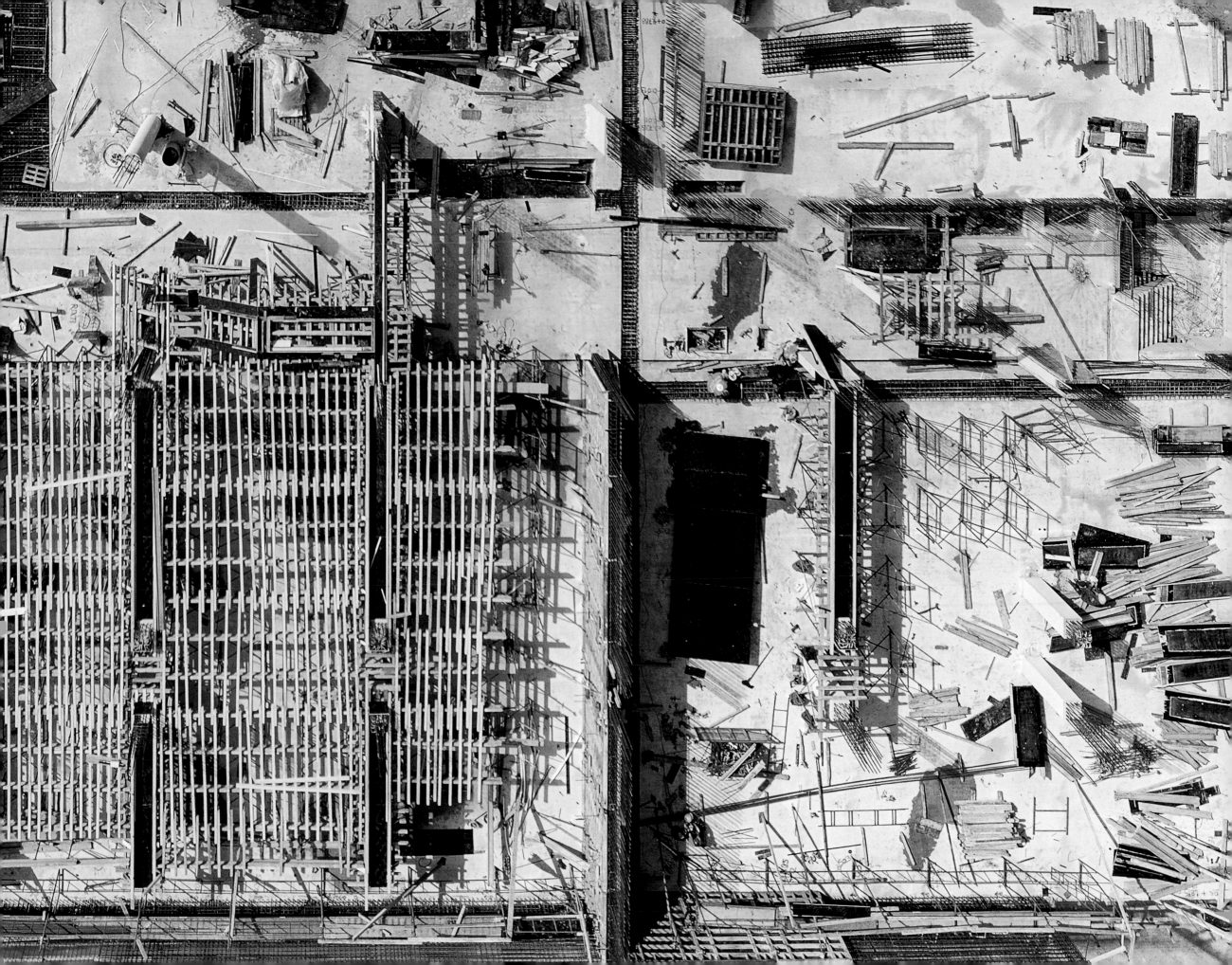

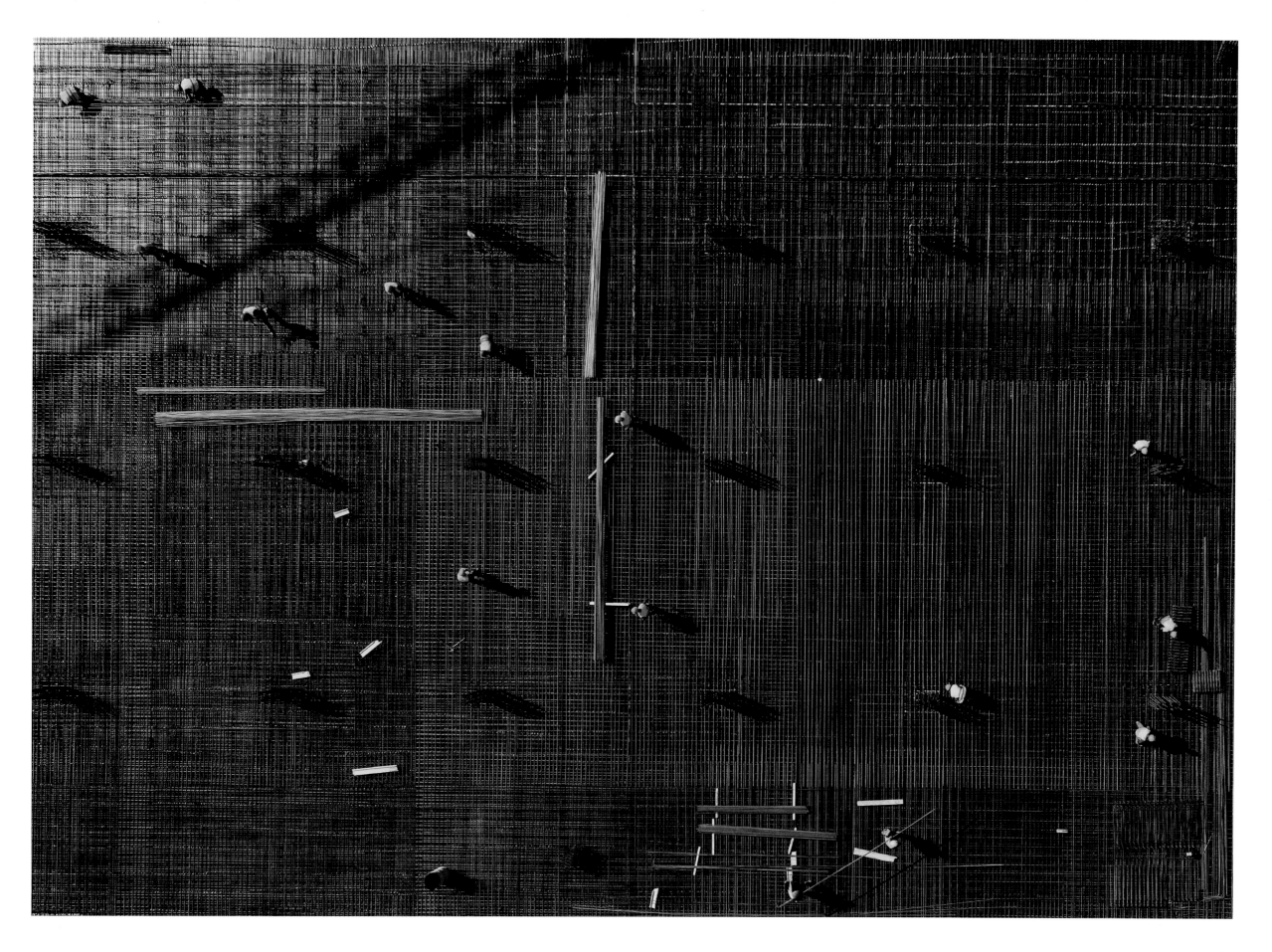

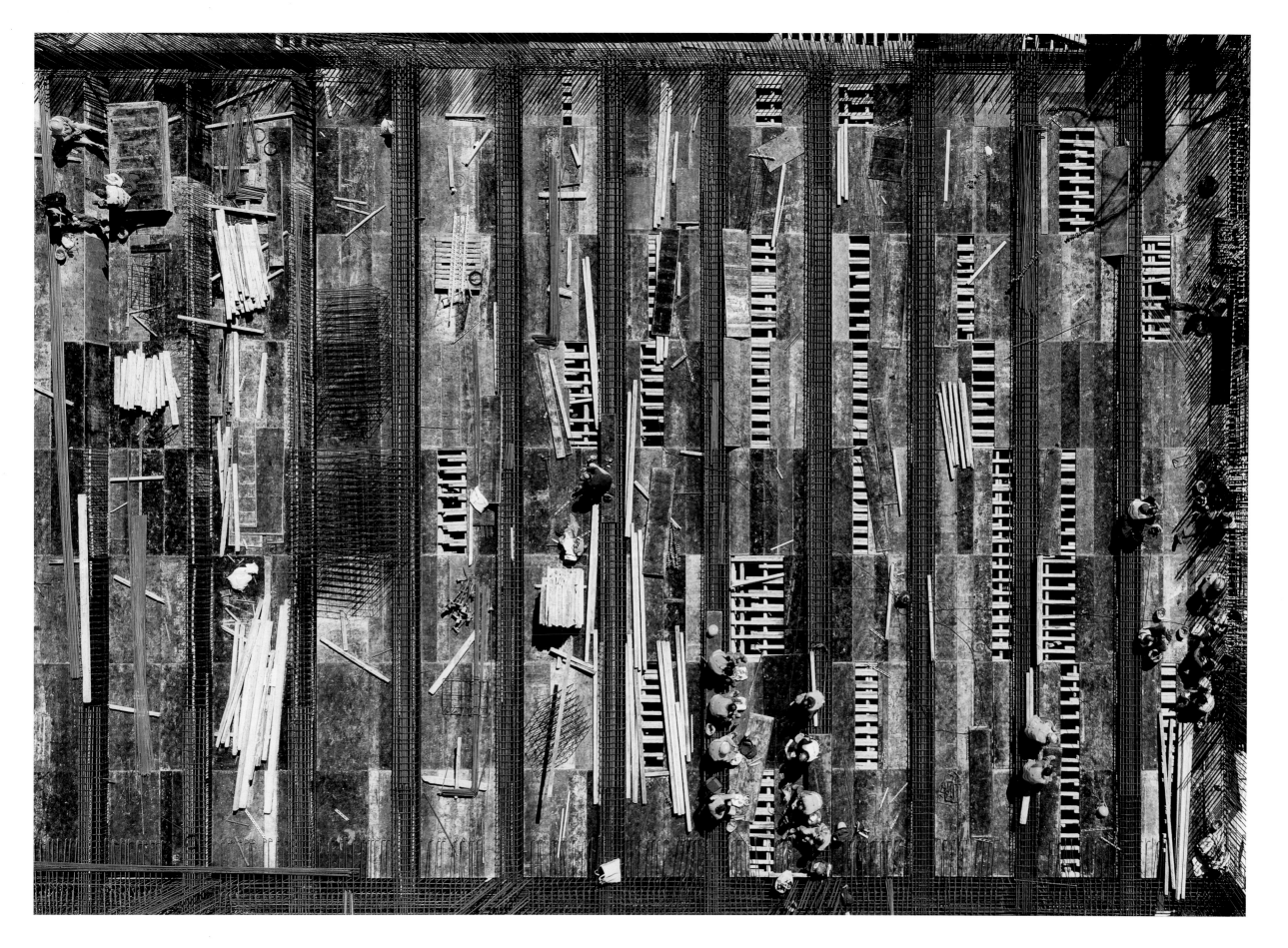

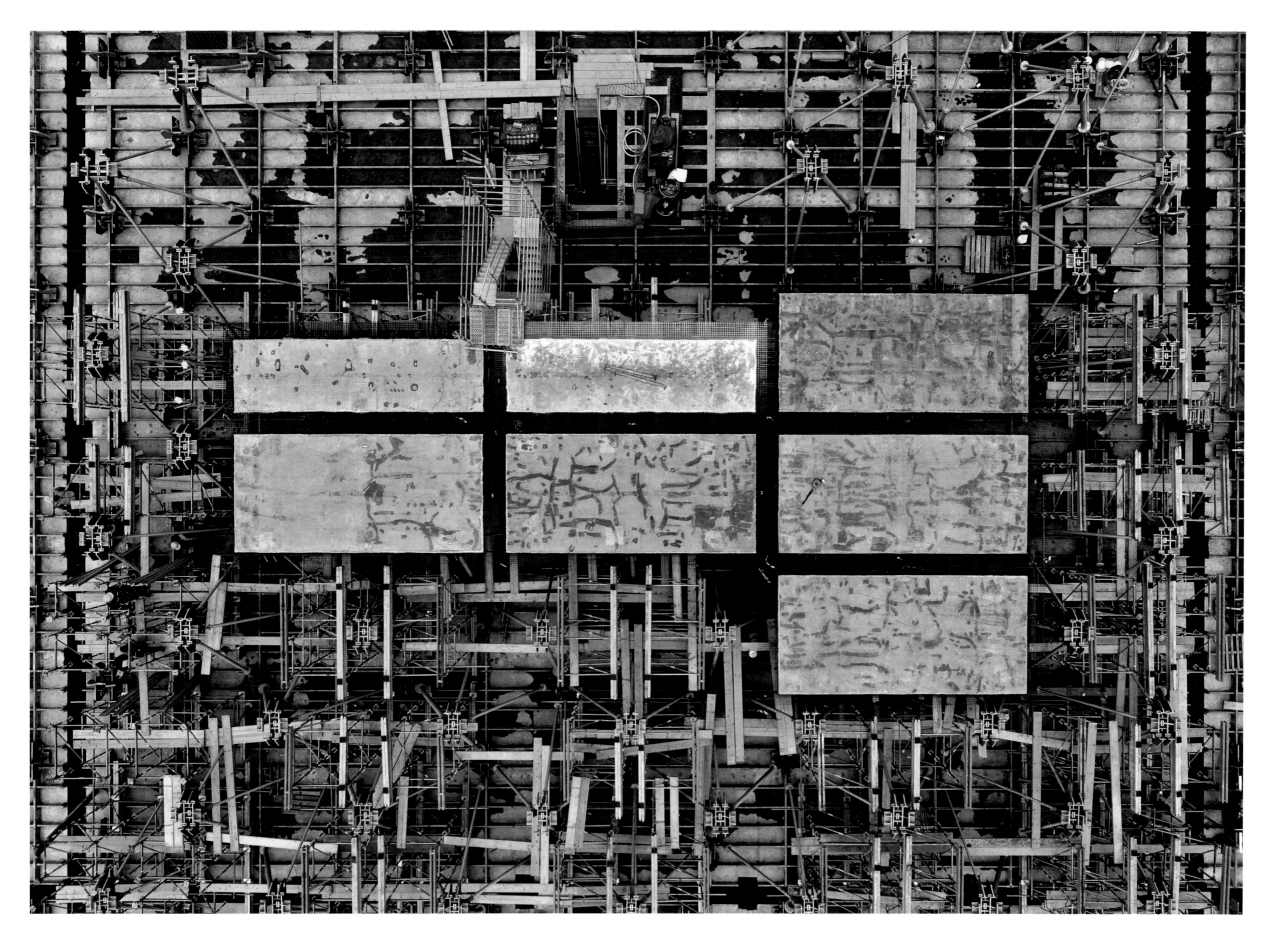

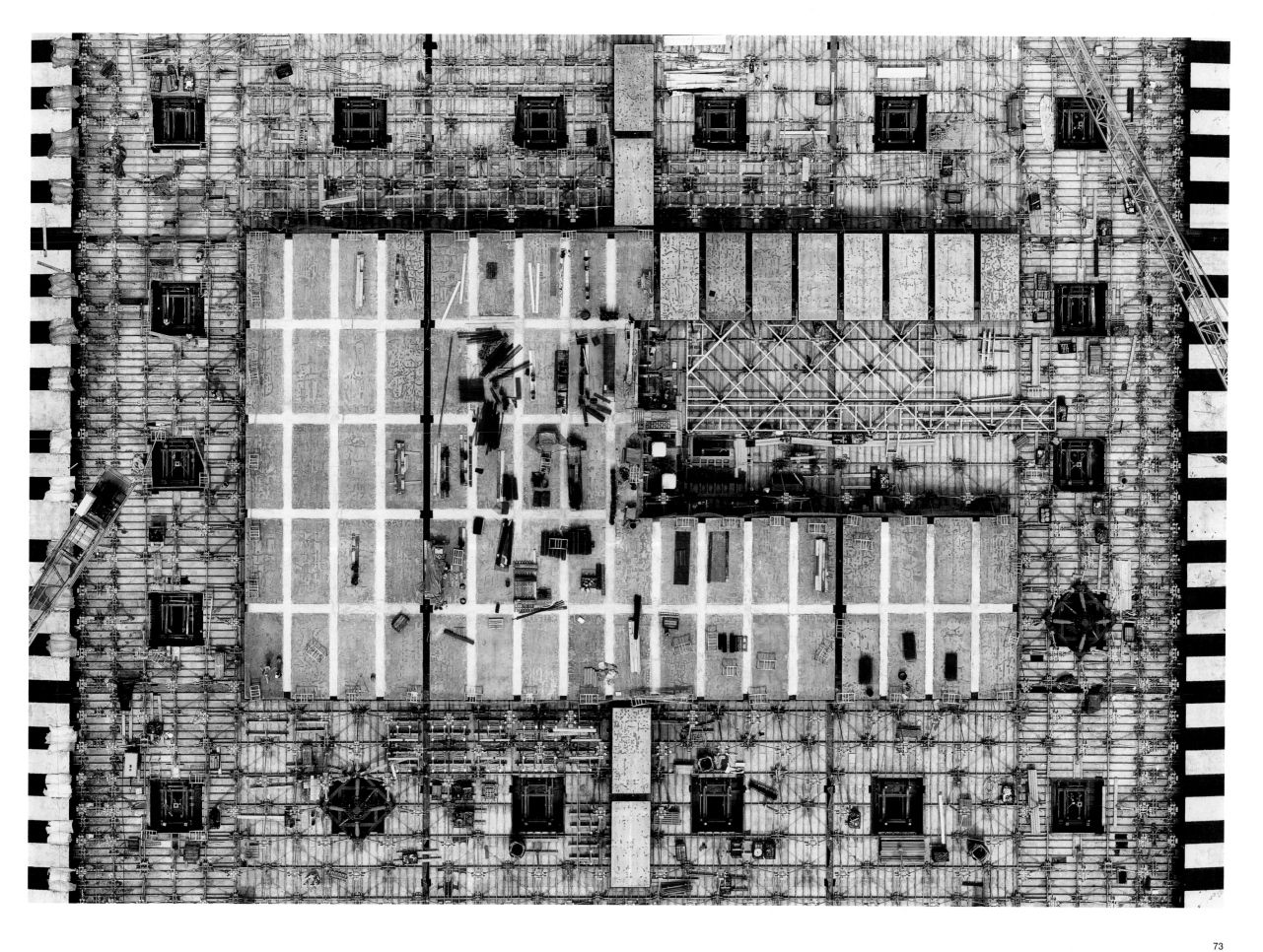

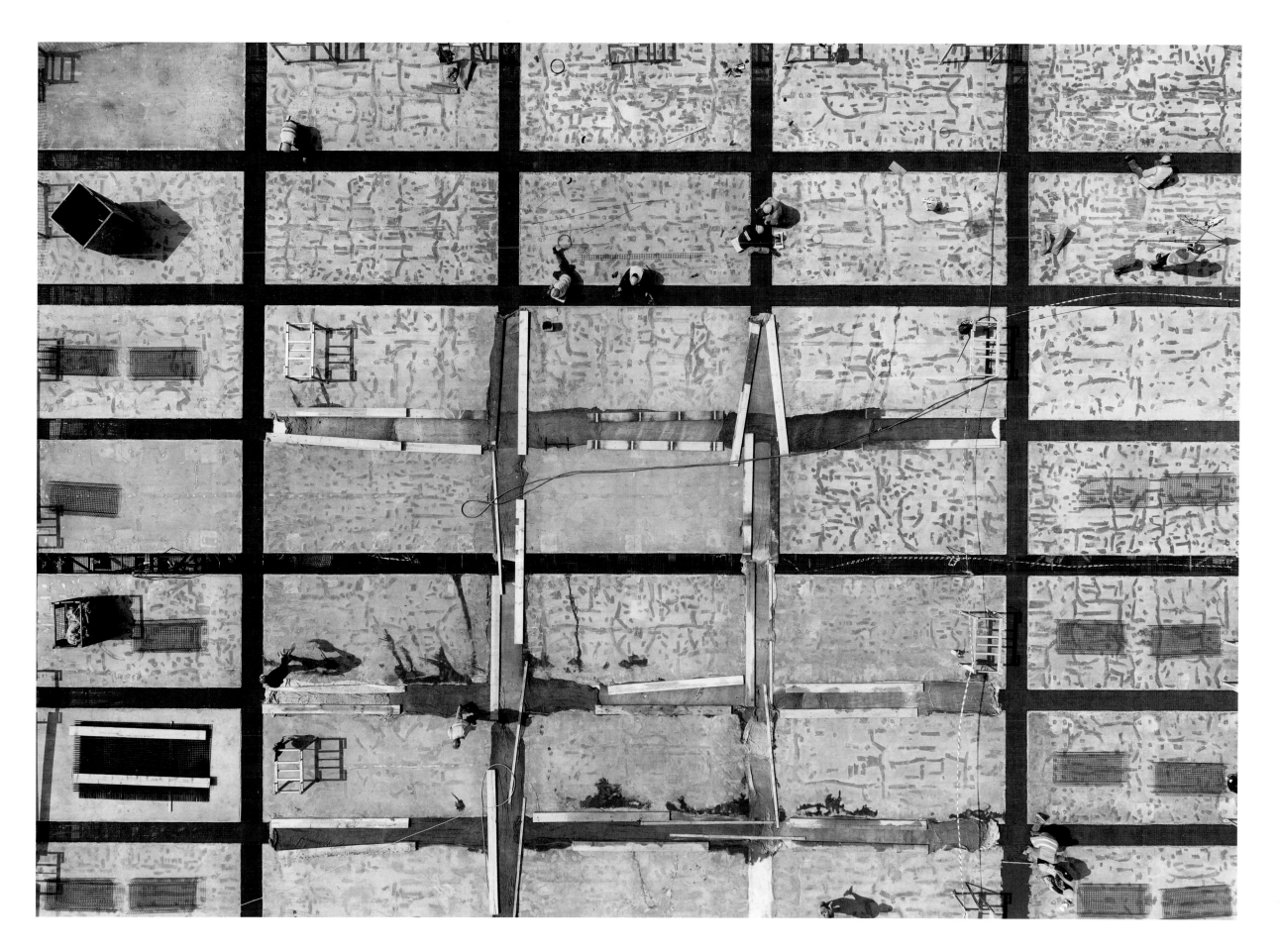

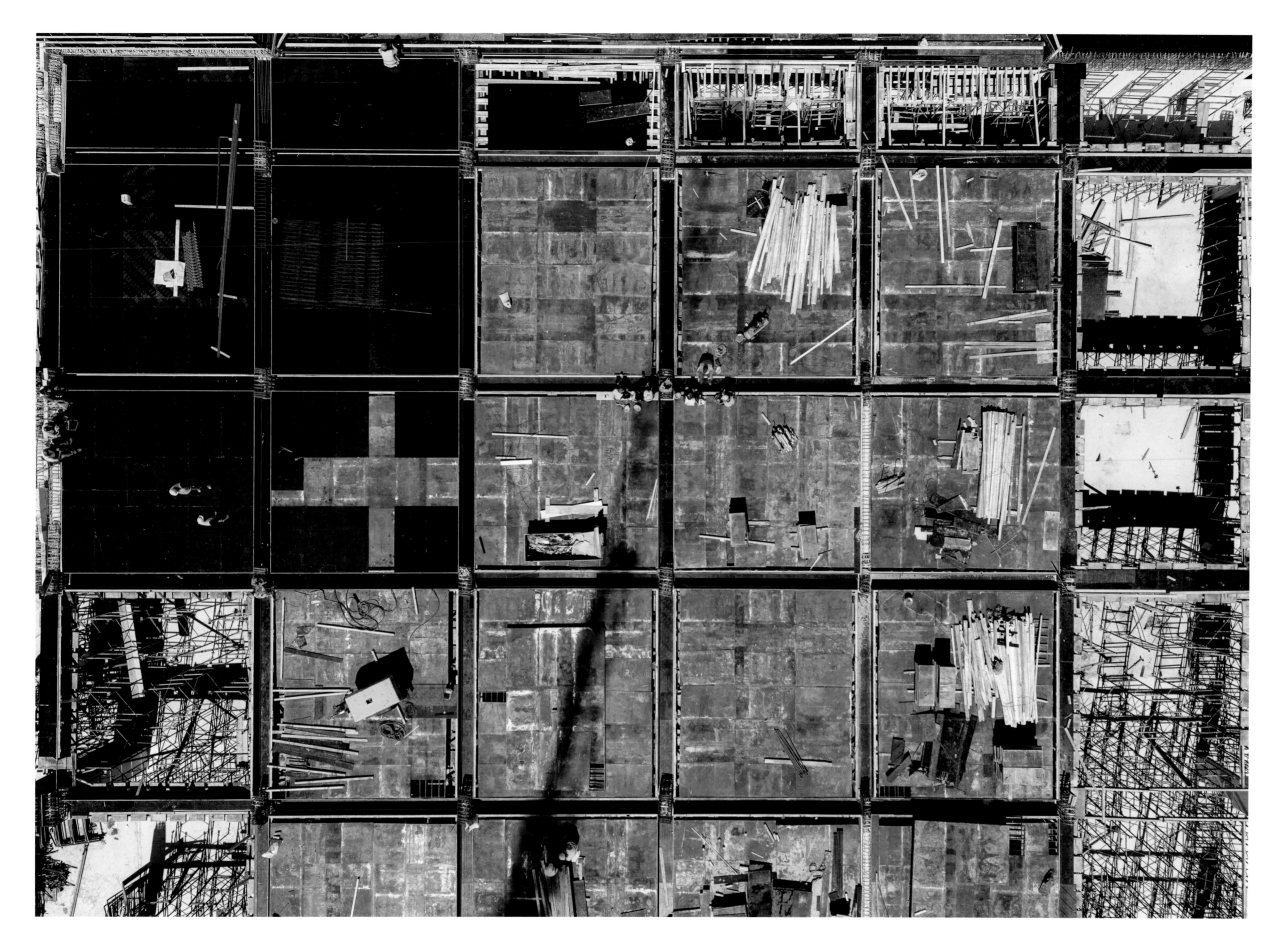

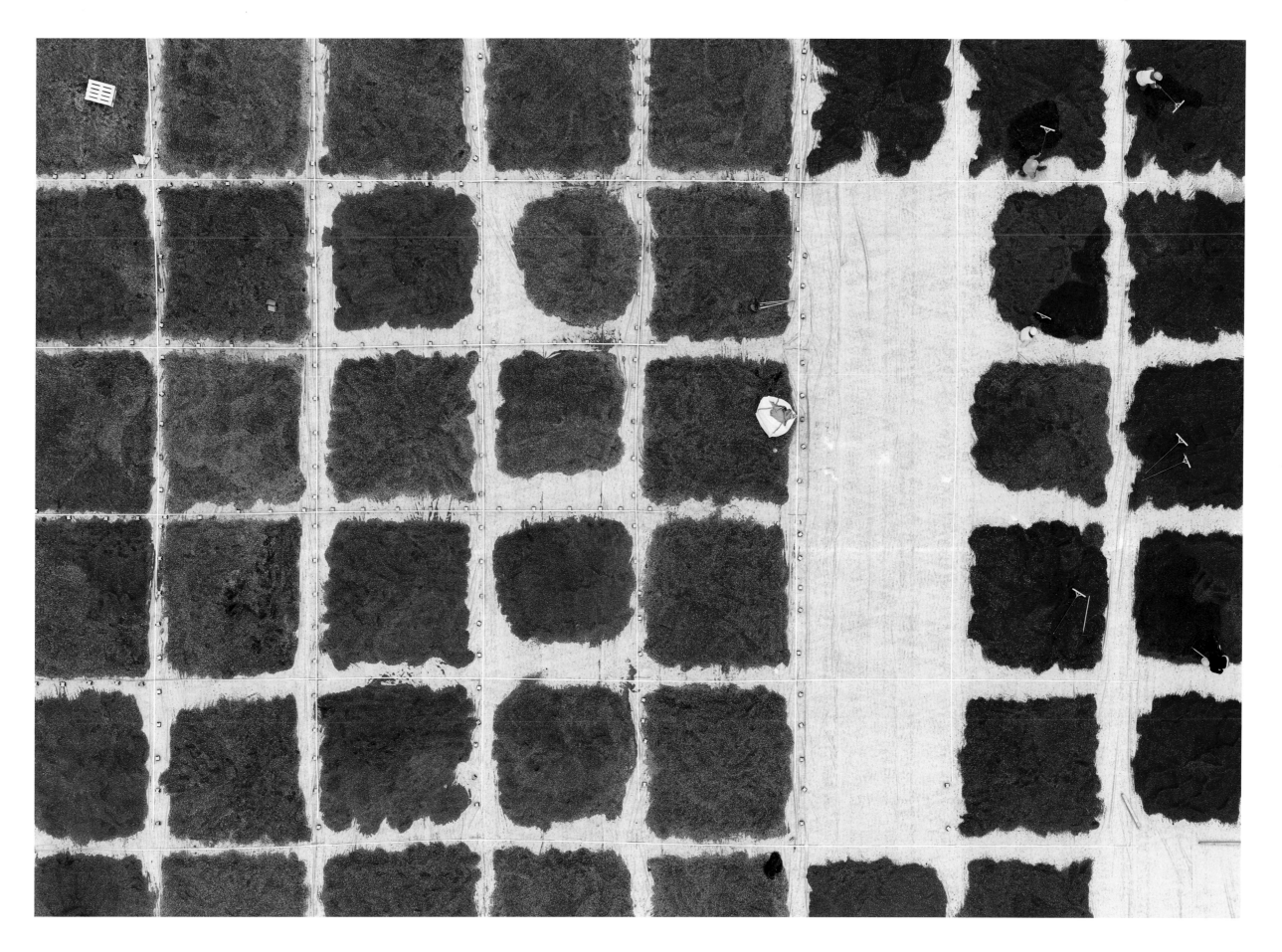

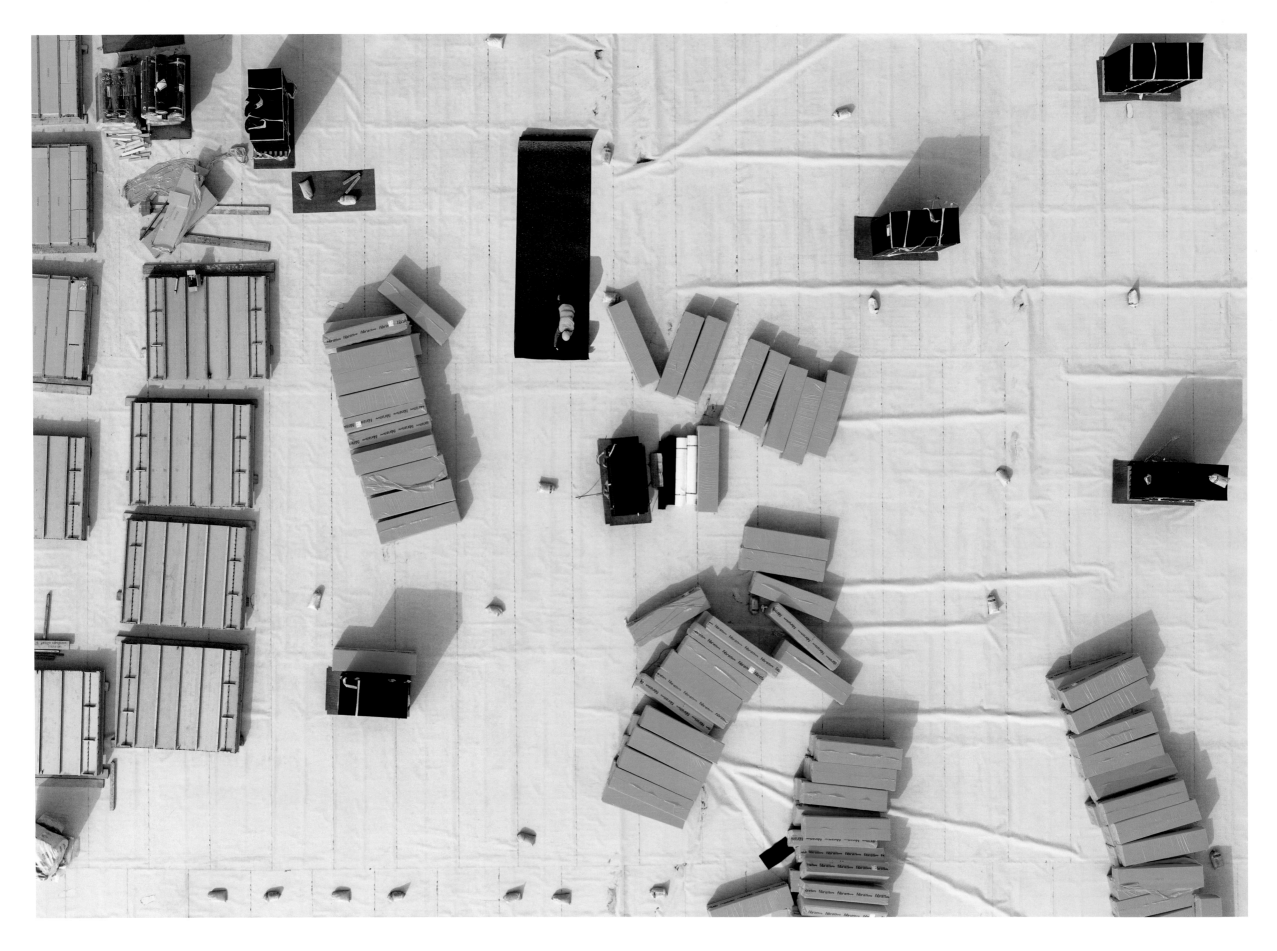

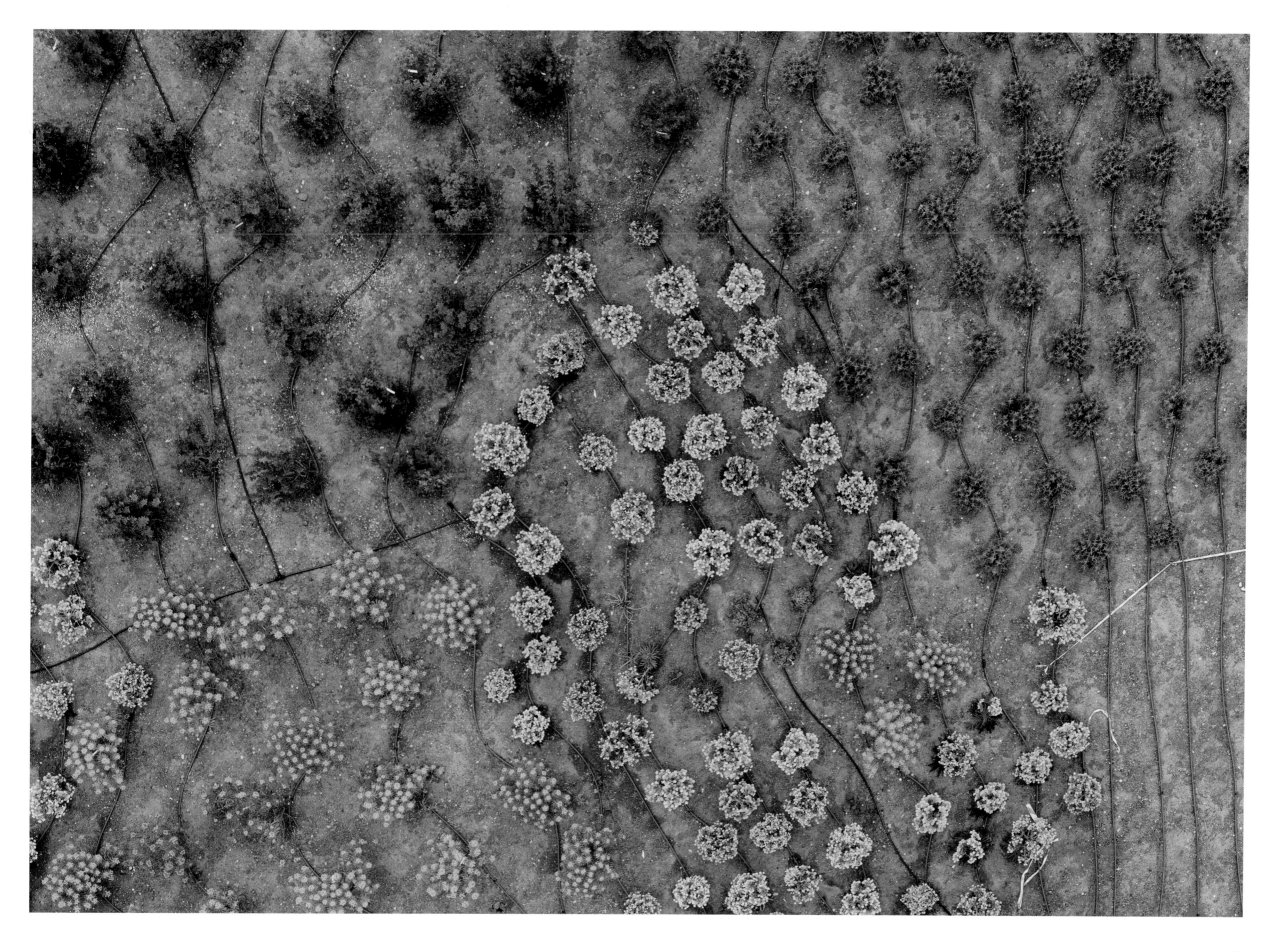

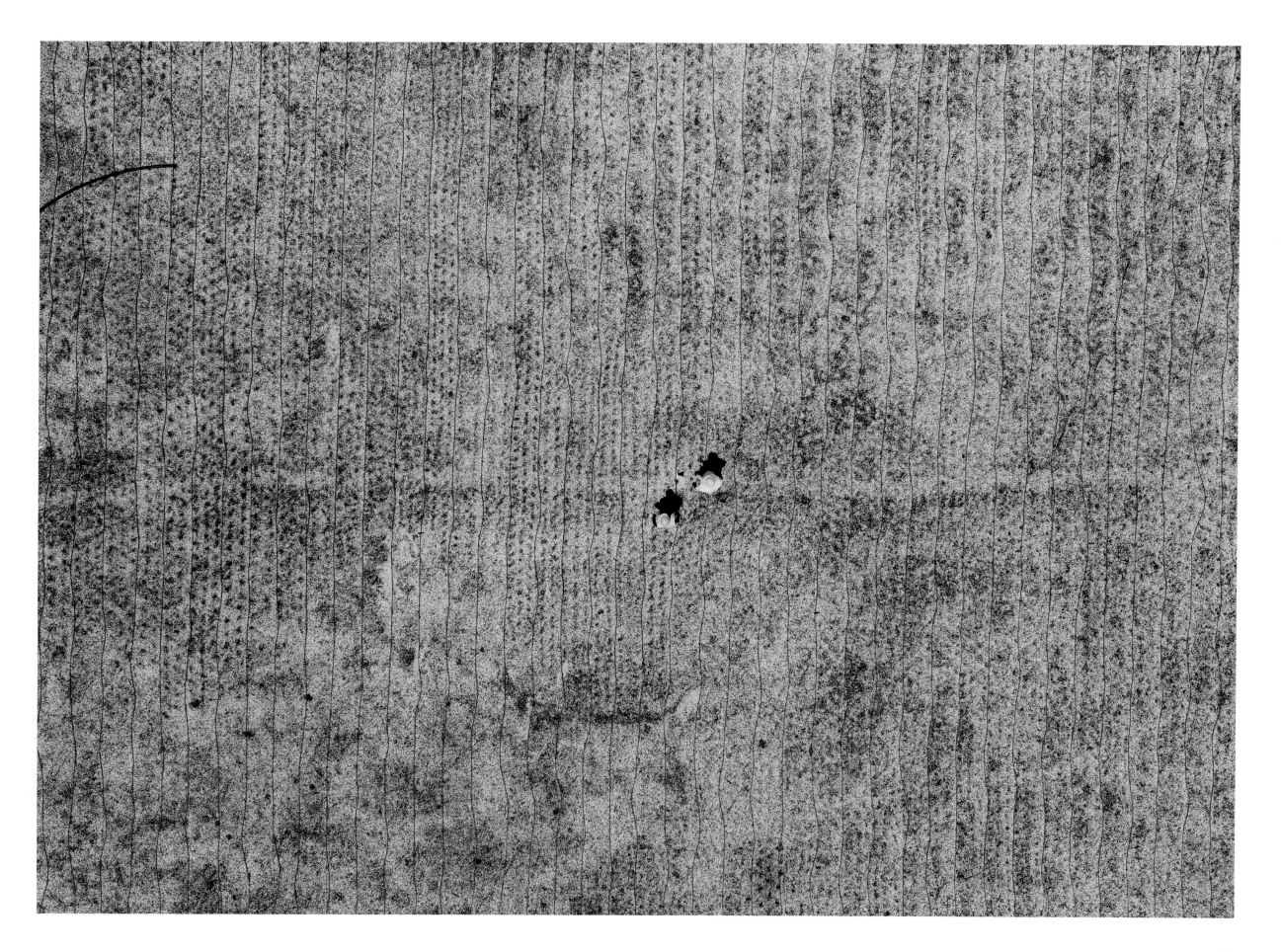

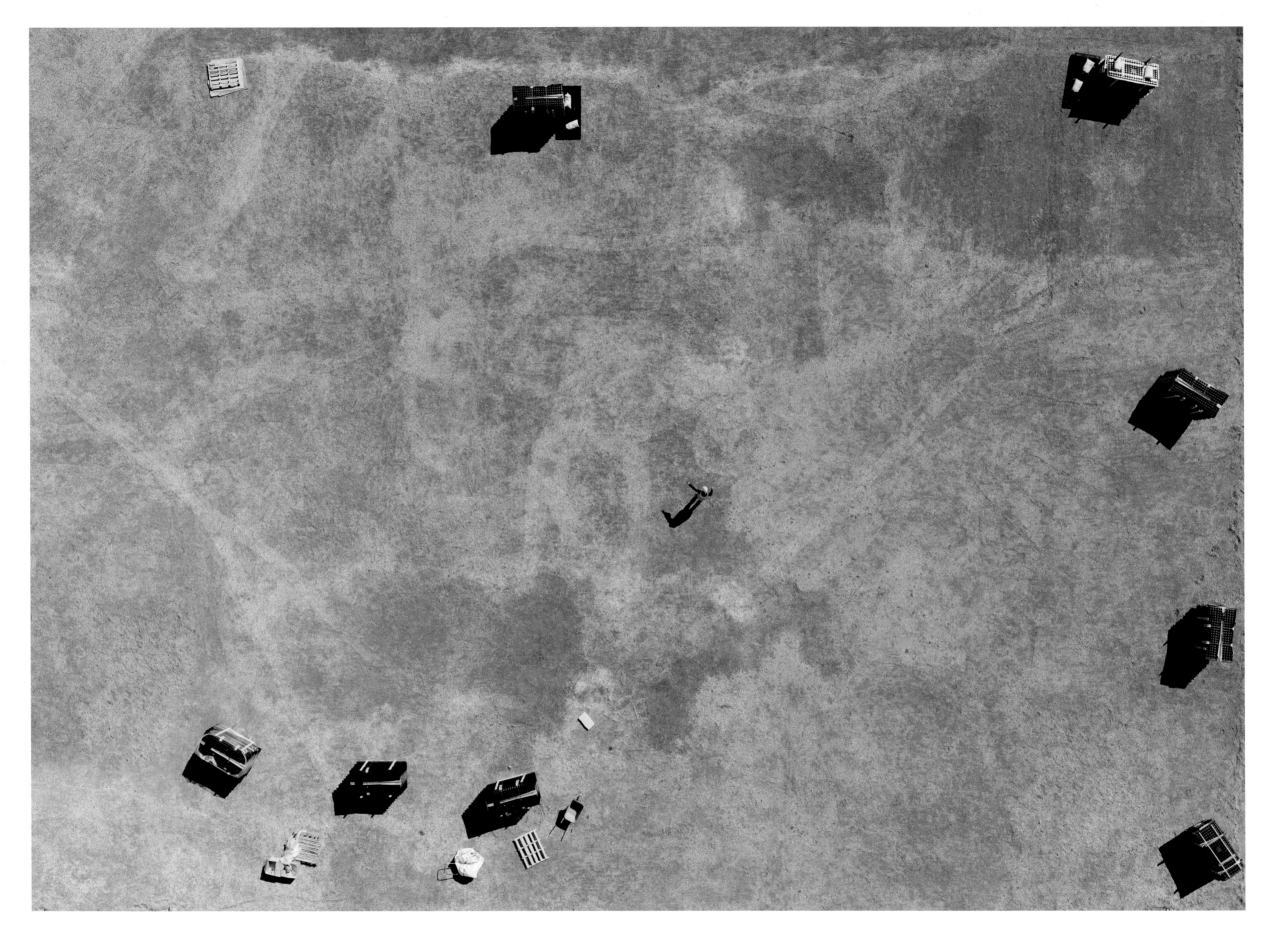

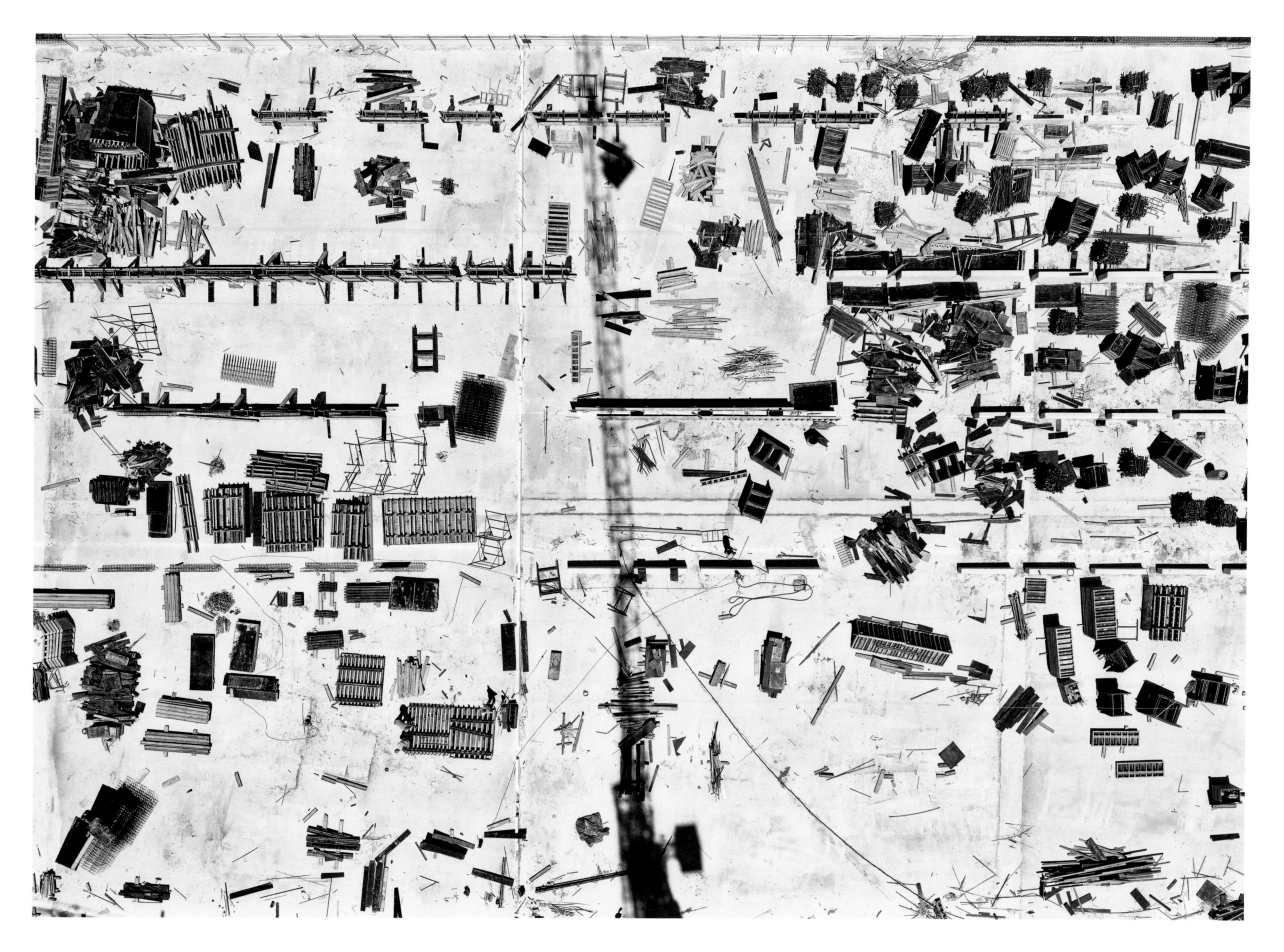

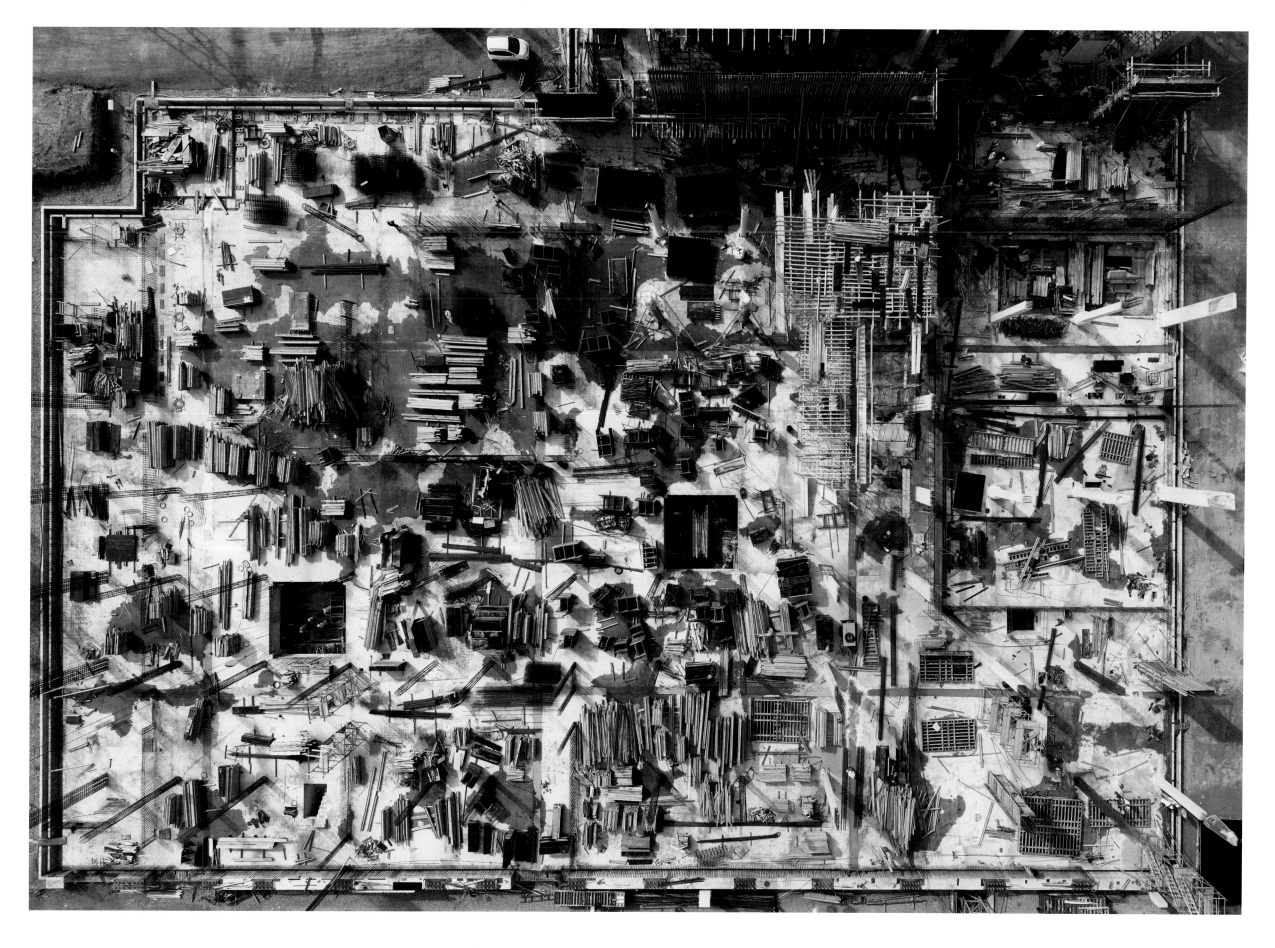

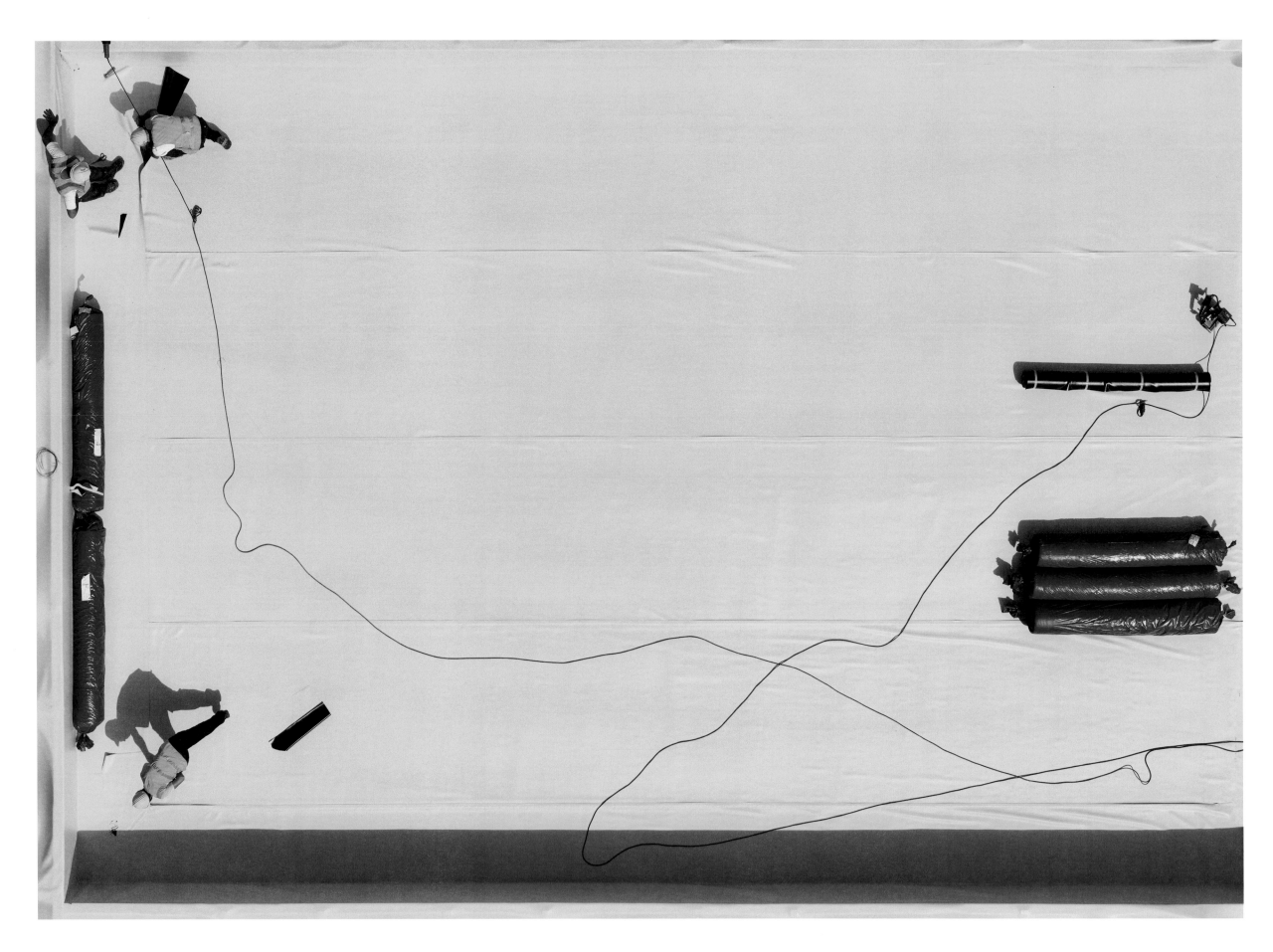

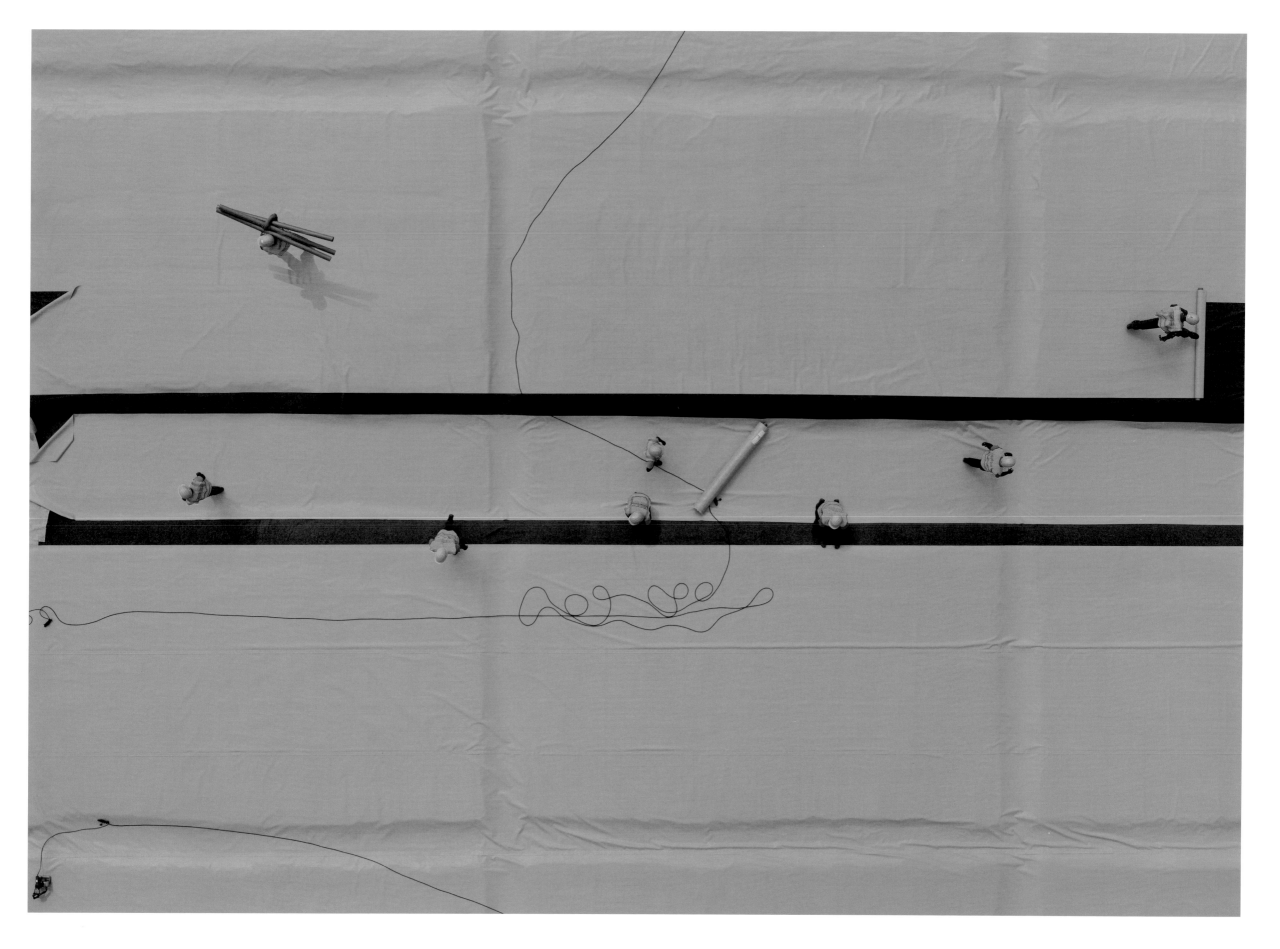

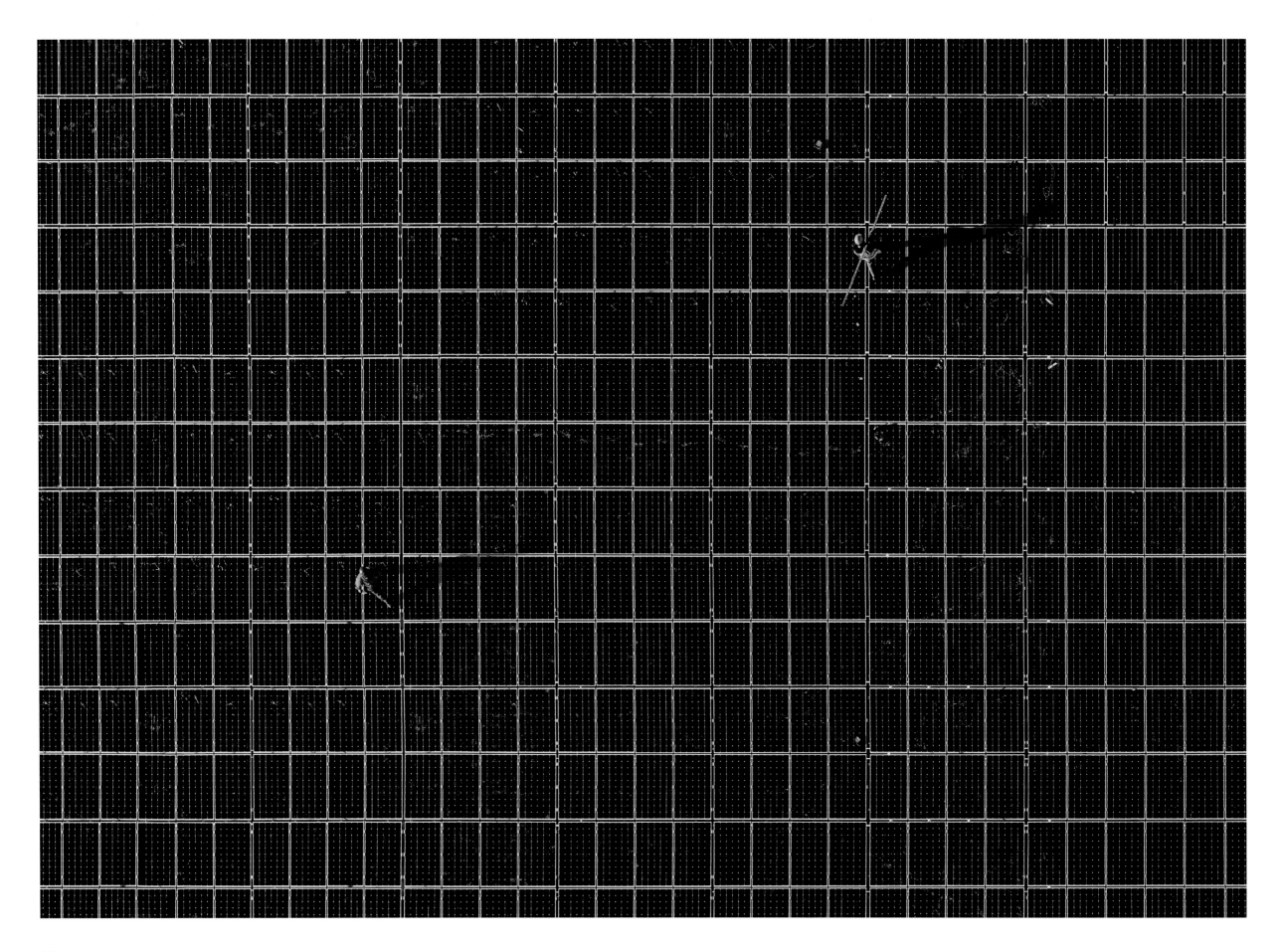

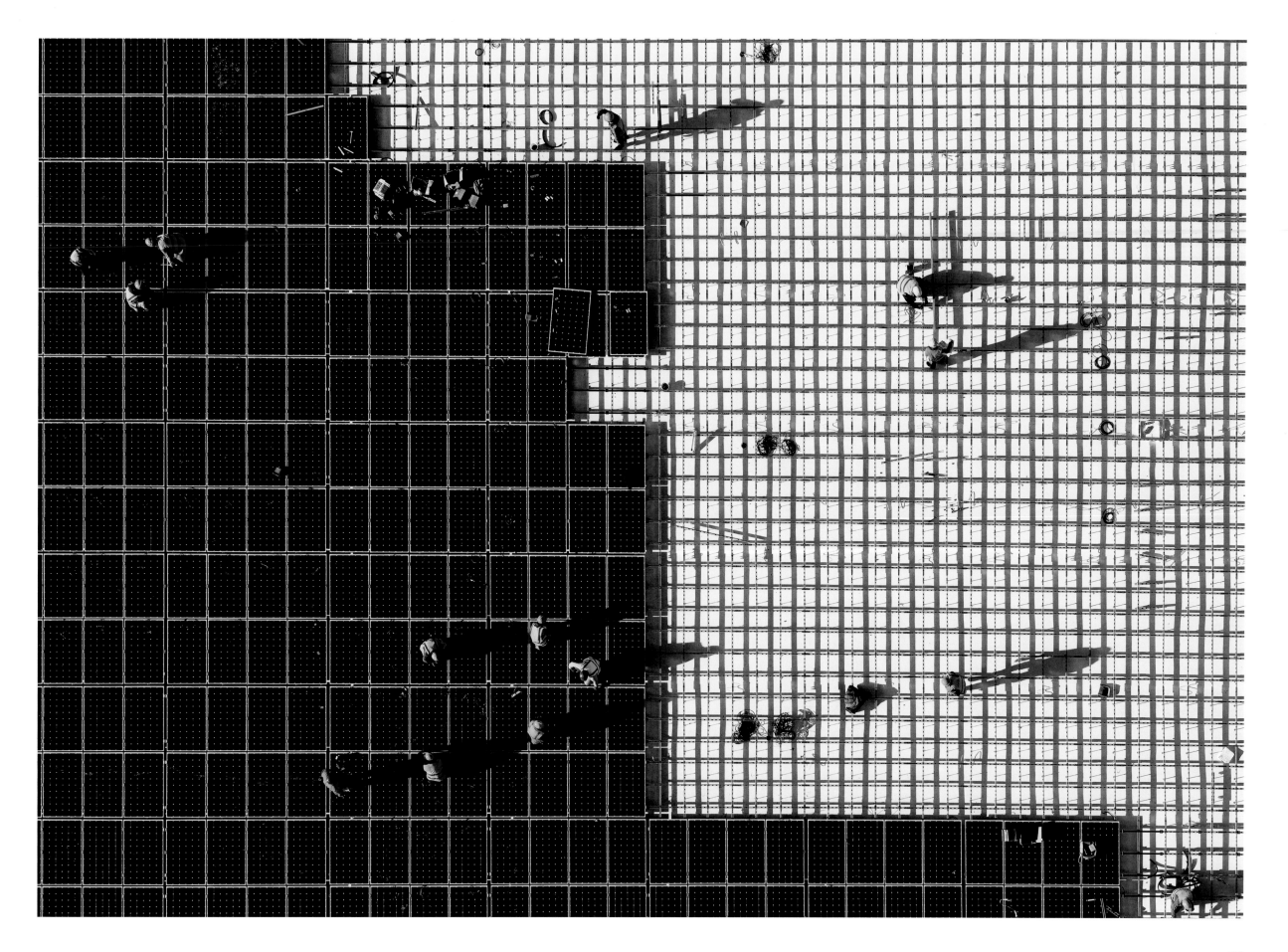

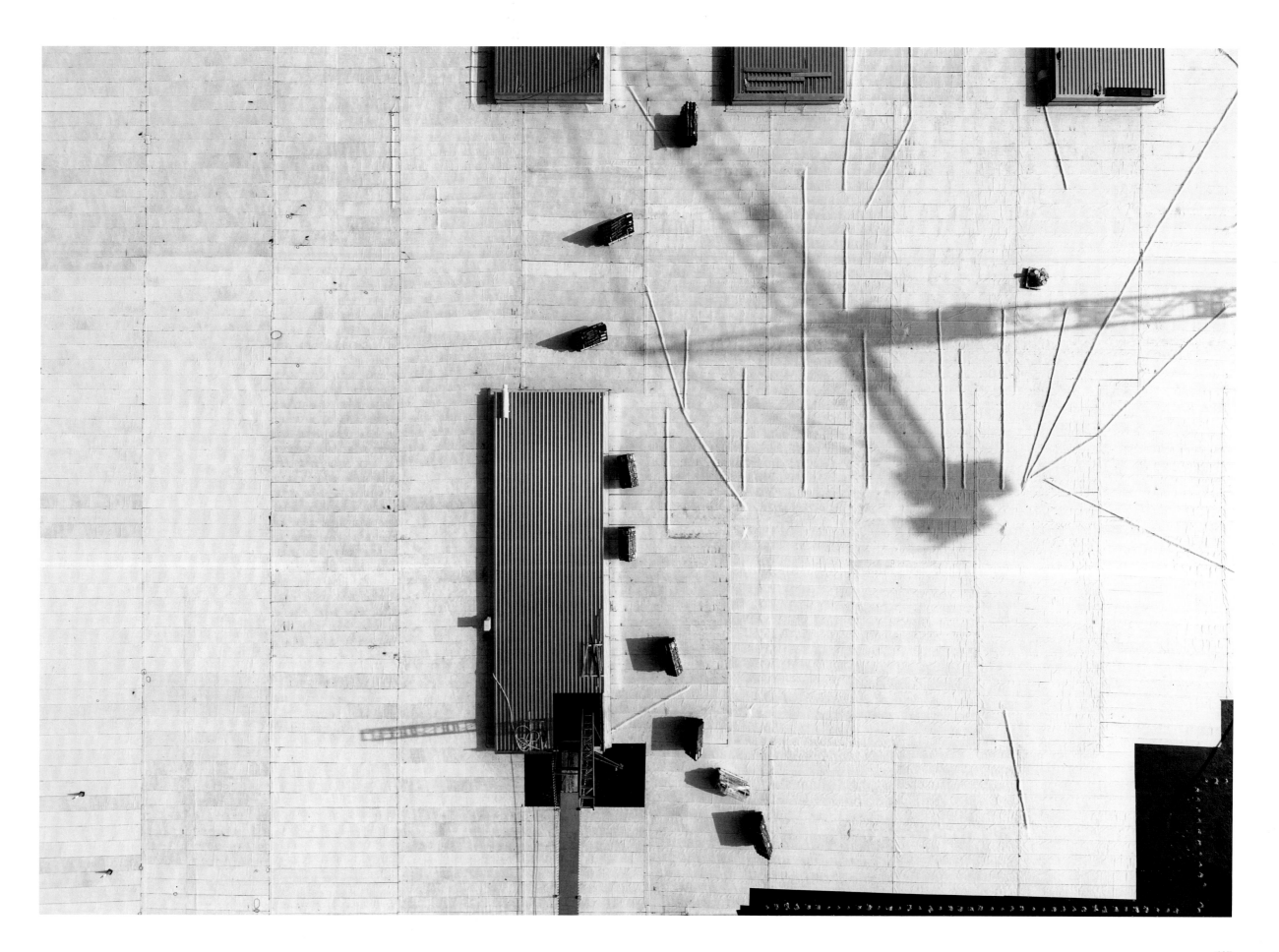

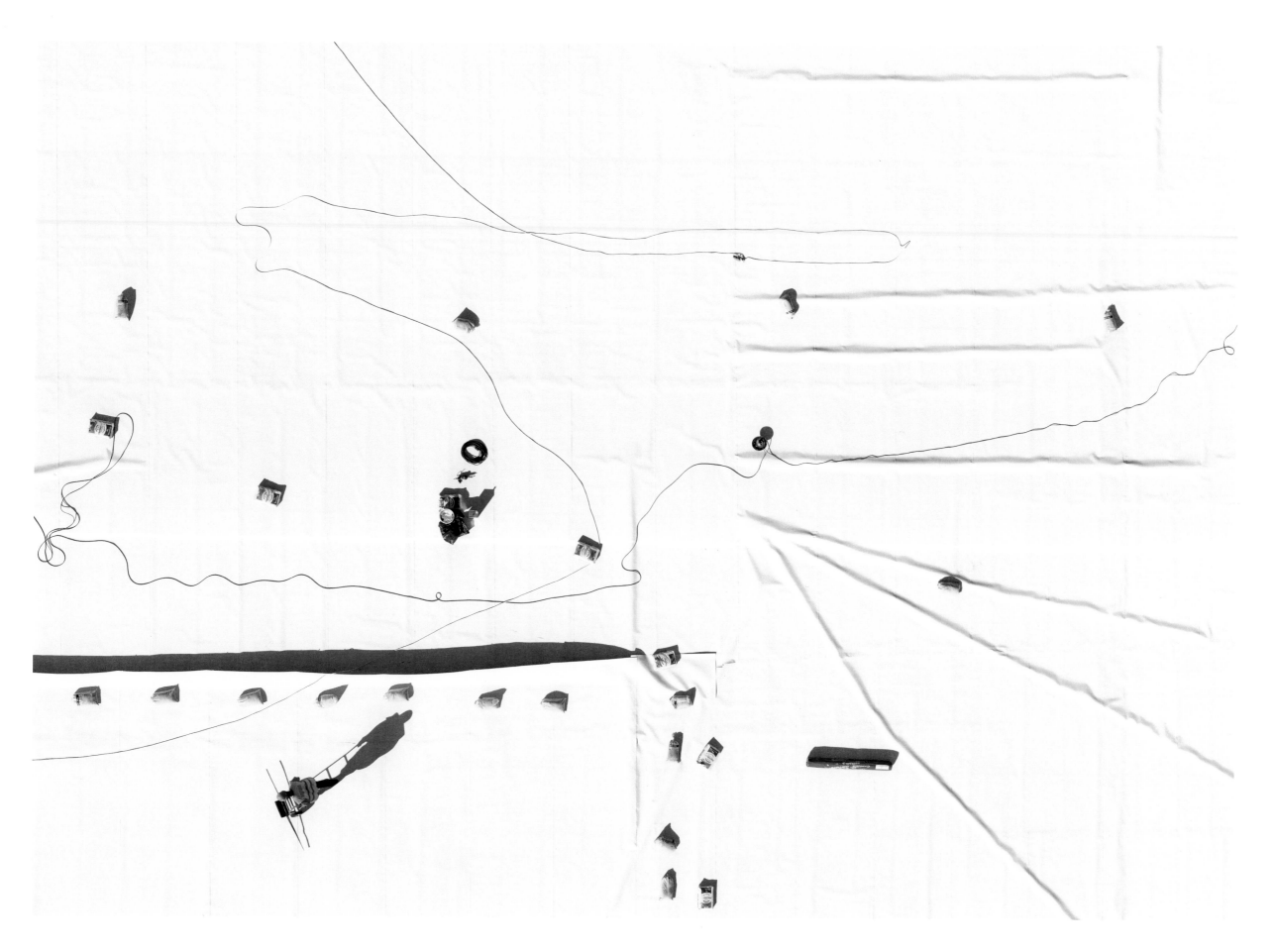

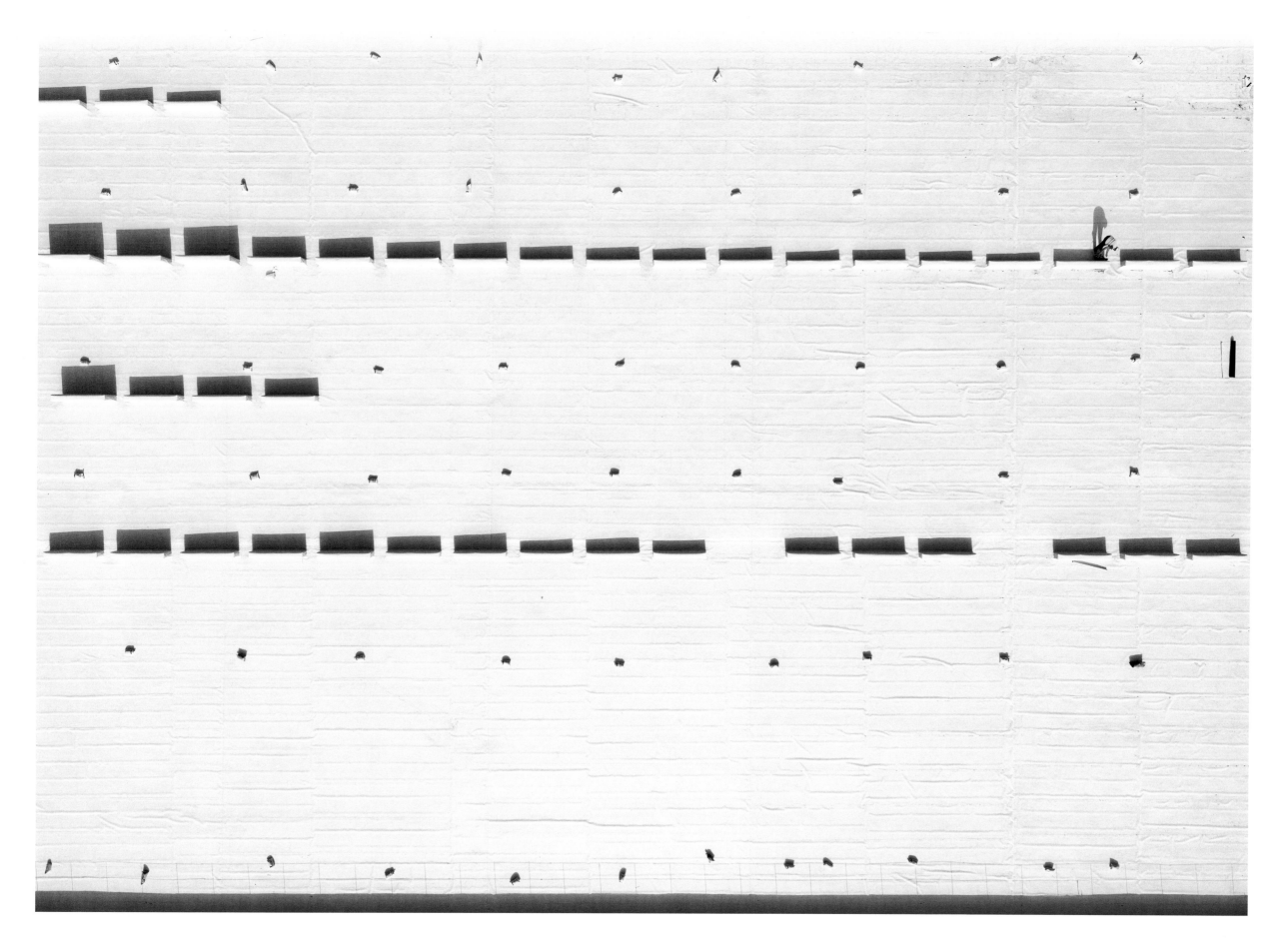

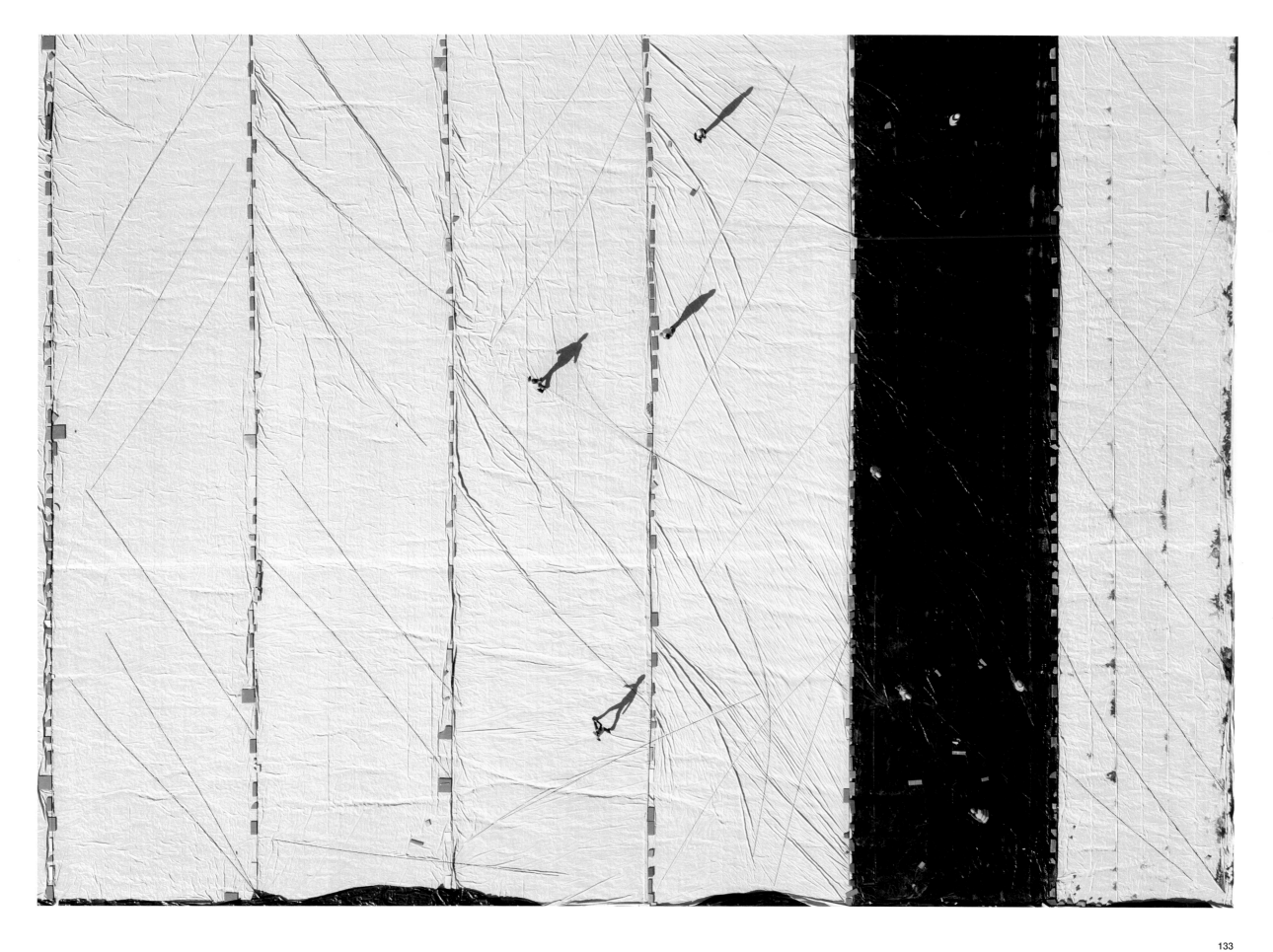

Orthographs

YIORGIS YEROLYMBOS

Landscape photography offers three verities: geography, autobiography and metaphor. What a landscape photographer traditionally tries to do is to show the past, present and future in one image.[1]

Robert Adams

I drive south, along the avenue linking Athens with the sea, passing the Acropolis. It is already late afternoon and I am heading toward the construction site on the Phaleron Delta for night shots.

Getting out of the car, I observe the Stavros Niarchos Foundation Cultural Center. The ground rises gradually from the park to the building, with the sun setting exactly behind it over the Port of Piraeus. The Canopy over the Greek National Opera seems to soar over the building like an airplane wing, slender and understated, while its lower side reflects the lights of the cars driving along the coastal avenue. The park is ready, the plantings are in, and the Canal is filling with water. Looking at the tiers of seats, I imagine them filled with groups of people under the plane trees, and at the same time I recall this space years ago, empty.

Each time I raise my camera to my eye, I see the present before me, I remember the past, and I think of the future.

I visited this site on the Phaleron Delta for the first time in June 2007, having been invited by the Stavros Niarchos Foundation to document the stages of this unique construction site photographically, as well as through the prism of my experience as an architect. The challenge of this commission was accompanied by anxiety: the qualities of the first sketches and models by Renzo Piano, the project's architect, gave the impression of a building complex that would be simple and in complete harmony with the place. But would the ultimate reality live up to the initial intentions? Over the nine-year period between the inception and completion of the work, I would have ample time to carefully observe each stage of its development, step by step.

On that first visit, the ground was covered from edge to edge with asphalt. The site functioned as an improvised parking lot for large vehicles in the morning and a racetrack in the evening. No matter where you looked, there were no views or vegetation, and the site was surrounded by noisy avenues. Human presence and scale were non-existent: it was a no-man's-land.

Since that time, slowly and steadily, without fanfare or tension, the landscape has changed radically. Hundreds of workers and engineers were installed and heavy machinery set to work, forever reshaping this place, transforming it gradually from a residual urban void to the city's cultural and artistic center.

Privileged to be a spectator in this world, I spent nearly a decade of my life at this construction site. I photographed it by day and by night, in winter and in summer, during the cold and in heat waves, alone and among crowds of workers. Of all the images that have been captured, one autonomous grouping stands out: the ground-plan photographs of the construction of the Stavros Niarchos Foundation Cultural Center (SNFCC), images that were created during my aerial orbits from the site's tower cranes. In my view, these are the most emblematic records of that ever-changing landscape; they respond in the most comprehensive way to the complexity of this vast project. For these reasons, I have chosen to show images exclusively from this body of photographs in the present publication.

The cranes were not always there, of course. The photographs I made during the earliest years of this project concentrated on the infrastructure and the preparations for the large-scale constructions that were to follow. The appearance of the tower cranes altered the landscape completely. Suddenly, the area claimed a third dimension. It took on *height*—and as such, begged the questions: How does it look from above? Might there be a reason to climb up there, and if so, how would one go about it?

Ascending the cranes took some getting used to. At first, I chose to climb their central column, following the lead of the operators who taught me how to do it. I climbed gradually, supported by both hands on the side rails, and made many stops as I got used to the altitude. After I had some experience, I began to go out along the boom, the horizontal beam that extends from the crane and lifts the loads. But looking down from that perspective, the largest part of my camera's frame was taken up by the crane itself, no matter how I angled the photograph.

The solution was to distance myself as much as possible from the vertical axis, going right to the edge of the boom. So I put on a safety belt, was harnessed to the metal basket, and, taking a deep breath, asked the crane operator to hoist me as high and as far out as possible. And there it was! The ground plan of the site appeared before my astonished eyes. With one eye on the camera viewfinder and the other on the level to ensure a position parallel to the ground, I began to make picture after picture without stopping, so as to not give myself time to think about where I was. I watched the workers while hovering exactly over them—at a height of 35, 80, or even 115 meters—and yet invisible to them, as they were all hard at work; no one glanced upwards. In each image I made, I used the basic lines of the building under construction in front of my lens as the axes of my composition.

With each "flight," I realized that the vision of the construction site from above was for me both a revelation and a relief. A revelation because the spectacle captivated

the gaze of the photographer in me, and a relief because the ordering of space through the ground plan organized everything in the mind of the architect in me. Suddenly everything fell into place, and the central approach of my own project became crystal clear: it would be a documentation and interpretation of the evolving landscapes of the construction site, following the vocabulary of architecture, but recorded in the language of photography.

What is my objective? That the photographs of the Center's ground plans render the intermediate, formative moments of architecture as visual events, maintaining their autonomy, each with its own significance and dynamic, preserving these moments from oblivion. For this to be possible, the images must strike a balance between the two disciplines they engage: they must be true both to the reality before them, architecture under construction, and at the same time to the art of photography. As the photographer Lewis Baltz—who largely created the approach that I follow—has said, photography must be consistent both with the world, which is the basis of science, and with itself, which is the basis of art.

Architectural photography and the ground plan as autonomous photographic subject are always on my mind, consciously or not, every time I lift my camera.

Architecture was of course a popular subject of early photography: from the very birth of the medium in the 1830s, photographers turned their attentions to buildings— stable, unmoving subjects well-suited to the slow speeds at which images were captured.[2] By the early the twentieth century, photographic techniques had advanced significantly, and numerous important architectural projects were photographed while under construction.[3]

Aerial photography made its first appearance in 1858 with the work of Nadar (Gaspard-Félix Tournachon), who made his images from a hot-air balloon. A century would pass before the first images from a satellite were published. Although technologies continued to advance, bringing new possibilities, photography from above was for many years generally limited to scientific uses, mainly for archaeological studies or military analyses. Aerial images were seen as important tools for transmitting information, but not for visual narrative. This began to change in the 1960s: aerial photography was used, for example, for Ed Ruscha's 1967 series "Thirtyfour Parking Lots in Los Angeles," which helped to secure the place of photography from above in the creative visual vocabulary.[4]

And the ground plan? Although used by builders since antiquity, the ground plan became an integral part of architectural studies during the Renaissance. Leon Battista Alberti was the first to describe the architect's drawing as distinct from that of the painter, arguing in his 1435 treatise *De pictura* that while both attempt to reveal depth, they follow completely different methods. The painter tries to conquer perspective with light and shading, whereas the architect emphasizes its agency by precisely following quantifiable, measurable data. In other words, the architectural drawing of a ground plan faithfully transfers to paper the depiction of a level in two dimensions, avoiding the distortions of the axes. The drawing in this way may serve as a "guide" for construction that liberates the creator-conceiver of the building from the laborer-builder. Alberti named such drawings "Orthographs."

In the photographs of the Stavros Niarchos Foundation Cultural Center, the effects of perspective are recorded with precision, and human scale is accounted for with consistency. My hope is that—just as the architectural drawing has its own life, separate and free from the bricks-and-mortar structure—my photographs may hold their own meaning as documents of this extraordinary building project, and perhaps something more. I cannot think of a way to more comprehensively describe these images than to borrow Alberti's title, "Orthographs."

During the construction of the SNFCC, I had the privilege of observing a landscape in transition. When the project is completed and opens its doors to the public, its users—lovers of music, readers, strollers in the park, families, and other visitors—will perhaps be under the impression that the place was always there in the form in which they see it. The successive stages of its construction and the human effort behind it will slowly fade from memory; the Center's functions will overshadow the ephemeral phases of its creation.

I look again at the completed building designed by Renzo Piano and it is clear that the reality fully validates the planners' initial expectations. My hope is that the photographs of the construction of the SNFCC will serve as a compelling record of the major changes that took place in this landscape before the dynamics of the final result made them self-evident—before they were taken for granted. Photographs, after all, have the power to transmit not only the news of the present day, but also the memory of the past and the anticipation of what is to come.

Athens, May 2016

1. The words of photographer Robert Adams that open this essay are from *California: Views by Robert Adams of the Los Angeles Basin, 1978–1983* (San Francisco and New York: Fraenkel Gallery–Matthew Marks Gallery, 2000).

2. Early practitioners who turned their lenses to architecture are William Henry Fox Talbot, Charles Marville, and Frederick Evans, among many others. Evans's iconic 1903 image known as *A Sea of Steps* is to my mind a perfect example of photography's ability to, in Robert Adams's words, "show the past, present and future in one image."

3. Perhaps the most emblematic of these photographic projects are Lewis Hine's documentation of the construction of New York's Empire State Building (construction completed in 1931) and Berenice Abbott's of Rockefeller Center (construction completed in 1933).

4. Aerial photography has been used creatively by numerous other artists over the years, including Mario Giacomelli, Olivo Barbieri, Frank Gohlke, David Maisel, Alex MacLean, Marilyn Bridges, and Jamey Stillings, to name just a few.

Timeline

The main elements of the design

The Stavros Niarchos Foundation Cultural Center (SNFCC) serves multiple functions. It is the site of the National Library of Greece and the Greek National Opera; it also comprises the Stavros Niarchos Park, a vast recreational space for public use, as well as a 400-meter-long Canal, and a Car Park. What follows are a basic outline of the principal design elements and an abbreviated timeline of the project's planning and construction.

Stavros Niarchos Park The Stavros Niarchos Park represents the physical link with Municipality of Kallithea at the northern borders of the project. Each area of the Park has a different planting scheme, creating a variety of climatic and aesthetic ambiences. The Park's layout is the work of landscape-designer Deborah Nevins.

The Park slopes gently upward from the northern end of the site toward the southern end. It gives the effect of a "tectonic movement" that has generated a new Hill. A large portion of this artificial Hill is landfill, while the rest, at the south, extends as a green roof on top of the buildings.

The boundaries of the Hill are defined by visible vertical concrete walls, dubbed the "Cliffs." At the northern boundary of the Park these are very low: 50 to 80 centimeters high; toward the southern end they reach a maximum height of about 32 meters.

To the west of the Hill, still within the Park, is the West Pedestrian Area, with a running track and workout equipment, shaded by trees: an ideal place for athletic activities.

The Canal and the Esplanade The Canal is a water feature east of the Greek National Opera and National Library of Greece buildings. Filled with seawater, it is 400 meters long, 30 meters wide, and a meter deep. The "banks" of the Canal are lined with long rows of trees.

The Canal runs parallel to the Esplanade, a pre-existing 40-meter-wide pedestrian walkway that was originally built for the 2004 Olympic Games. The Esplanade connects the city of Kallithea with the coast over the busy Poseidonos Avenue. The SNFCC project includes new plantings and hardscaping over the Esplanade area.

The Main Building and Agora The SNFCC's Library and Opera functions are designed as one central building. The main entrances of both the Library and the Opera are accessed from the Agora, a 40-by-40-meter open space that extends north to the Library lobby, south to the Opera lobby, west to the public spaces connecting the two institutions, and east in the direction of the Canal. All building elevations facing the Agora are covered from ground level to roof level with custom-designed glass façades.

Inside the Library lobby solid concrete walls enclose special reading rooms and exhibition spaces. This structure, called the "Book Castle," is surrounded by a system of light-access balconies and bookshelves. From the Library lobby visitors may reach the Greek National Research Library or the Greek National Library, as well as exhibition spaces; business centers; special reading areas for adults, teenagers, and children; and a radio station.

Inside the Opera lobby a similar but larger concrete volume encloses the Main Auditorium space. Five levels of balconies surround the structure, providing access to the various levels of internal Opera tiers.

The Opera lobby gives access to the 1,400-seat Main Auditorium, as well as the 450-seat Performance Hall 2 (also known as the Alternative Stage), which is south of the Auditorium. The performers' entrance is located on the south side of the building.

The Canopy and the Lighthouse The Canopy is the architectural landmark of the project. It is a 10,000-square-meter light structure located on top of the Opera, at the southern end of the Park. It hovers like a concrete "flying carpet" (in the words of Renzo Piano), providing shade to the Opera roof and the Lighthouse area below.

The Canopy structure is made of light steel bracing members covered on top and below by a thin shell made of ferro-cement—a reinforced cement-mortar material—and supported by 30 thin steel columns, which are directly connected to the concrete structure of the Opera's roof.

Functionally, the Canopy it is not a roof but a collector. The energy of the sun is captured through the 5,560 photovoltaic panels installed on the shell of the Canopy, generating 2.0–2.2 gigawatt hours (GWh) of energy per year, which is directed to the internal project grid and provides credits

to the overall Leadership in Energy and Environmental Design (LEED) accreditation.

The SNFCC project aims to earn the platinum "green"-building LEED certification, the first such distinction in Greece, and the first for a public building of this scale and complexity in Europe. LEED is an internationally recognized green-building certification system, providing third-party verification that a building or community was designed and built using strategies intended to improve performance in metrics such as energy savings, water efficiency, CO_2-emissions reduction, improved indoor environmental quality, as well as stewardship of resources and sensitivity to their impacts.

The Lighthouse is a glass-enclosed pavilion on top of the Opera and directly under the Canopy. This multifunctional public space can be expanded to its balcony and the panoramic steps of the Opera's roof, offering magnificent views over Athens.

October The Stavros Niarchos Foundation (SNF) announces its intention to fund the planning, construction, and outfitting of the SNFCC, including new buildings for the National Library of Greece and the Greek National Opera, and a Car Park building, all surrounded by a twenty-hectare outdoor cultural, educational and recreational space comprising the Stavros Niarchos Park, the Agora, the Canal/Esplanade area, and access roads.

June The SNF signs a "memorandum of understanding" with the Greek State, initiating the SNFCC project.

July Consultants conduct needs analyses and execute program requirements for the project. Extensive geological and hydrological investigations are undertaken to confirm the suitability of the site, a former equestrian area used as a parking lot during the 2004 Olympic Games, for the development of the SNFCC.

February After an invitational international architectural competition, the SNF's board of directors selects Italian architect Renzo Piano and his team, the Renzo Piano Building Workshop (RPBW), to design the Center. The co-presidents of the Foundation's board of directors, Andreas Dracopoulos, Philip Niarchos, and Spyros Niarchos, along with Renzo Piano and the project's director, Giorgio Bianchi, meet with Greece's Prime Minister Konstantinos Karamanlis to apprise him of the project's progress.

April Feasibility studies begin. The SNF will closely follow the development of these studies at regular monthly meetings at the RPBW offices in Paris.

October The first schematic designs are drawn up.

January The Foundation's board of directors and RPBW present the concept design for the SNFCC to Prime Minister Karamanlis and representatives of the Greek State at the Zappeion Hall in Athens. A public presentation follows at the Athens Music Hall. The newly designed SNFCC logo combines blue (the national color of Greece), turquoise (representing the Greek seas), and green (for new green space, the Stavros Niarchos Park).

March The SNF signs a contract with the Greek State for the construction of the SNFCC. On behalf of the State, the contract is signed by Greece's Ministers of Economy and Finance, Environment and Public Works, and Education and Culture, as well as by representatives of the National Library of Greece, the Greek National Opera, the Hellenic Public Real Estate Corporation, and Olympic Properties S.A.

July The Greek Parliament ratifies the contract between the SNF and the Greek State, paving the way for the start of construction.

Project consultants develop designs under the close supervision of Renzo Piano.

June Presentation of the final architectural plans and related technical studies to the public at the SNFCC site. The event is attended by 3,500 visitors. In addition to Renzo Piano's presentation, attendants have the opportunity to visit specially designed exhibition spaces, with detailed information on the architect's plans for the three principal functions of the SNFCC: the National Library of Greece, the Greek National Opera, and the Stavros Niarchos Park.

December Preliminary excavation work and archaeological research commence.

December 20, 7:00 a.m.: Ground is broken at the site.

The bidding process begins for the selection of a construction firm.

September The main construction contract is signed between SNFCC S.A. and a joint venture of two major specialized contractors: Salini Impregilo from Italy and Terna from Greece. The construction schedule outlines three interim milestones and a final-deadline goal for the project. Phase 1: completion of buildings' foundations (within twelve months). Phase 2: completion of aboveground concrete works (within twenty-two months). Phase 3: completion of the Canopy (within twenty-eight months). Phase 4: the construction project is to be completed within thirty-eight months.

October Major construction activities begin with the building of temporary site facilities and general excavations. Earth is moved to form working platforms, enabling the installation of concrete piles for the foundations of the buildings, and gravel piles for stabilizing the ground under the Hill.

February Full-scale load tests are conducted on sample locations at each of the three main buildings (Opera, Library, and Car Park). The results of the tests are used to confirm or fine-tune structural designs and to gauge final adjustments to the pile lengths. After the load tests, the casting of concrete piles begins for all main buildings.

Also in progress: concreting diaphragm retaining walls at the perimeter of the Opera house stage pit, and installation of gravel piles under the retaining wall at the perimeter of the Hill.

June Installation of seismic isolators begins. These innovative devices, installed between the concrete superstructure and the foundations, are designed to reduce the effects of seismic movements and enhance the structural and architectural integrity of the Opera and Library buildings in the case of earthquakes (common in Greece). Each type of isolator has undergone a full-scale dynamic test, conducted at specialized testing facilities (at the Università di Pavia, Italy, and the University of California, San Diego) following European regulations. Upon successful completion of testing, a certificate is issued for their use.

Also in progress: concreting of ground-level slabs for the Opera and of the final group of piles for the Library and Car Park, and installation of geo-grids (reinforced-earth structures) retaining the backfill at the perimeter of the Hill.

August Construction of the storm-water-management network begins at the Hill area. The storm-water drainage strategy for the project addresses two needs: first, avoid overloading the existing public networks with high peak rates of storm-water runoff from the project area; and second, protect the project area from internal flooding. The basic means to achieve these objectives are the sustainable urban drainage systems (SUDS) installed at various locations on the Hill, in compliance with LEED requirements. The SUDS comprise infiltration trenches combined with new-technology "geo-cellular boxes." These boxes provide a final infiltration step, serve as buffer storage, and release excess storm water to the public networks at controlled, significantly reduced rates.

September 28 The first interim phase of construction is complete. The foundation structures, including concrete piles, pile caps, and the foundations for Opera, Library, and Car Park buildings are finished.

October The temporary Visitors Center, located on the Esplanade, opens its doors to the public. This building is designed by Greek architecture students Spyridon Giotakis and Agis-Panagiotis Mourelatos, who were selected by Renzo Piano through a nationwide student competition. The plans for the Visitor Center's interior were supervised by exhibition-designer Erato Koutsoudaki and her team.

Between October 2013 and January 2016, this Visitors Center will host more than three hundred events and welcome more than 58,000 visitors.

November The Opera stage pit concreting is completed, as is the overall ground slab for the Opera and Library buildings. Concreting of the Car Park's first floor and the walls around the Hill is in progress.

January After many mockups and much research and testing of materials at local and international laboratories, production of the ferro-cement elements for the Canopy begins at an onsite facility. The process requires numerous special elements and techniques, from the mesh reinforcement to the composition of the mortar, which is injected into custom-designed steel molds. The 717 ferro-cement elements needed for the project will be produced over a period of a year by a team of around two hundred technicians.

February The concrete works for the building superstructures are underway, with the Car Park and the structures for the Maintenance and Waste ancillary buildings at the Hill reaching their final stages.

May After the installation of the primary irrigation network, topsoil is deposited on the Hill. The first olive tree is planted in the Mediterranean Gardens on May 23. By June, 97 trees are planted in the Mediterranean Gardens, on the Great Lawn, and near the northeast entrance of the site.

    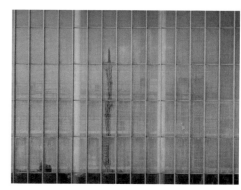

After the hot summer period, planting resumes: between September 2014 and May 2015, some 568 trees and 62,000 shrubs are planted. The final planting period is from September 2015 to May 2016. Ultimately 1,400 trees, 128,000 shrubs, 165,000 plug plants, and 21,700 bulbs are planted on the grounds of the SNFCC.

All plants in the Park are species native to the Mediterranean area; most of them are of Greek origin. The plants selected are drought tolerant, requiring moderate quantities of irrigation water.

June 25 The SNFCC, still under construction, hosts its first choreographed dance performance, in the area of the Stavros Niarchos Park. The "performers" in this innovative dance are the ten construction cranes that have been working daily on the SNFCC site. The fifteen-minute performance begins just before sunset: the cranes move rhythmically to the music of Gustav Holst's *The Planets*, performed live by the Greek National Opera Orchestra, under the baton of Myron Michailidis (artistic director of the Greek National Opera). This unique spectacle, titled *The Dance of the Cranes*, is the inspiration of Renzo Piano.

The performance brings the SNFCC to life, demonstrating to the attending public that the complex will serve as a cultural and educational fulcrum for Greece.

July 28 Phase 2 of construction is complete: the concrete frames and slabs for the Opera, Library, and Car Park buildings are finished. The Opera's concrete roof slab is ready to accommodate the tall, heavy-duty scaffolding required for the erection of the Canopy.

Also in progress: the concrete façade walls for the Opera and Library; internal "box-in-box" structures for acoustically insulated rooms; interior walls; electromechanical works inside buildings; hardscaping on the Hill (installation of curbs and concrete channels).

September 4 With scaffolding now erected, the installation of the 717 prefabricated ferro-cement elements and the bracing steel structure of the Canopy begins.

The construction of the Canopy will take eleven months, advancing through a series of milestones: the bottom ferro-cement shell (April 23); the internal steel structures (April 29); the steel columns and column-head assembly (May 26); the top ferro-cement shell (June 12); the casting of the joint zones between the prefabricated elements (July 25); and the final completion of the Canopy structure (August 8).

The completion of the ferro-cement structure is followed by the application of the protective coating and the installation of the photovoltaic panels on the top shell.

November 17 After the construction of concrete façades to the building elevations, the placement of the glass-façade sections begins.

The glass façade is a custom-designed structure spanning from the ground to the roof level. This transparent structure surrounds the Opera and Library lobbies facing the Agora and the Canal, extending to the Opera Restaurant and Lighthouse, creating a sparkling exterior sheath.

The process of erecting this façade takes place over a period of sixteen months; installations are completed in the following order: Opera, north side (December 18, 2014), Opera, east side (March 31, 2015), Library, south side (April 4, 2015), Library, east side (June 19, 2015), Opera Restaurant, level 5 (October 10, 2015), Agora, front and back (December 12, 2015), and finally the Lighthouse (March 3, 2016).

Many parts of the SNFCC are completed during the course of this year: the Cliff structure (January); acoustic wall panels in Performance Hall 2 (February); floating floors in Opera rehearsal rooms (April); marble floor in Library lobby (May); Car Park epoxy floors and Canal concrete structure (June); splash fountain in the Park area on the Hill (July); timber floor for Library lobby balconies (August); removal of Canopy scaffolding (September); marble floor in Opera lobby and timber floor in Performance Hall 2 (October).

June 21–24 After three years of ongoing construction work, the SNFCC invites the public to visit the complex with a program of events focusing on four themes: arts, sports, education, and sustainability. Over the course of four days and nights, the Stavros Niarchos Park welcomes approximately forty thousand visitors with performances and activities in a range of fields: music, photography, architecture, athletics, the environment, creative workshops, and night-time screenings of video art.

The Foundation's goal with the annual June Events is to communicate the philosophy of the SNFCC: open and accessible to all, it is a hub where the arts interact with recreation and sports, scholarship and nature.

More elements are installed toward the end of 2015: acoustic wall panels in the Opera rehearsal rooms; timber floor in the Opera lobby balconies; dome and ring in the Main Auditorium; Car Park green roof (November); timber floors in rehearsal rooms (December).

January Wooden interior-wall panels are erected in the Main Auditorium; seats are installed in Performance Hall 2; and a mast is erected on top of the Canopy. Rising 40 meters above the Canopy (80 meters from ground level), the mast is a flexible antenna-like element that moves in the direction of the wind.

February The timber floor is laid in the Main Auditorium seating area, and Library bookshelves are installed.

March Seats are installed in the Main Auditorium; glazed partitions are placed in offices; the Library's green roof and the Opera's green roof are completed.

The photovoltaic panels are installed.

June 23–26 The SNFCC again opens its doors to the public with four days and nights of cultural events, in a program titled *Metamorphosis: The SNFCC to the World*. It includes performances and more by world-renowned artists from Greece and abroad, and an innovative program of cultural, sports, and educational activities for all ages.

Some 115,000 visitors have the opportunity for the first time to enter the new premises of the Greek National Opera and National Library of Greece, as well as to enjoy the Stavros Niarchos Park. The SNFCC continues to be established to the public as a place of ideas, exploration, and experimentation.

Index of Plates

Canal bottom concrete, construction joints (p. 21)

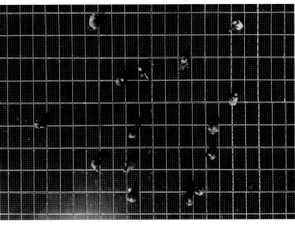

Photovoltaic panels on top of Opera Canopy (p. 22)

Opera Canopy, application of protective coating to upper surface (p. 23)

Hill, at the start of earthworks (p. 25)

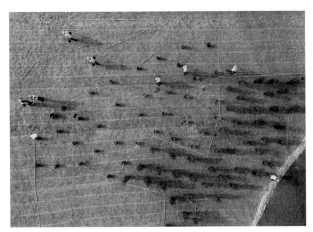

Hill, planting of trees (p. 27)

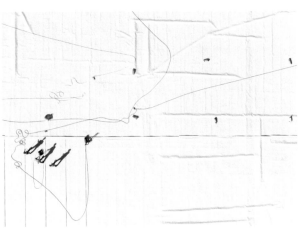

Library, roof waterproofing (p. 29)

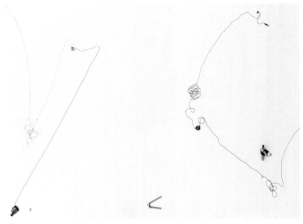

Car Park, roof waterproofing (p. 31)

Canopy top surface, ready for installation of photovoltaic panels (p. 32)

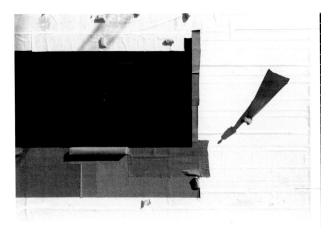

Car Park, roof waterproofing (p. 33)

Car Park, roof waterproofing (pp. 35–37)

Canopy top surface, before application of protective coating (p. 38)

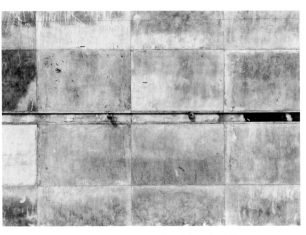

Canal bottom concrete, construction joints (p. 39)

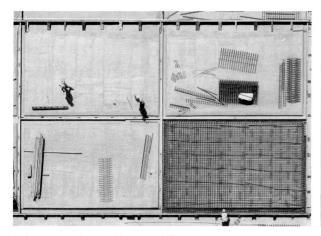

Reinforcement to the Canal (p. 40)

Concreting the Canal (p. 41)

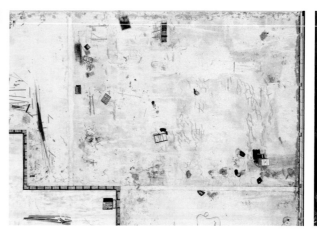

Car Park, concrete roof slab (pp. 43–45)

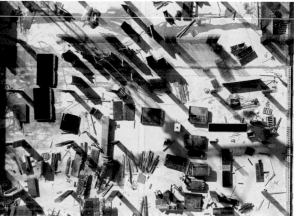

Library, ground-level slab (pp. 47–49)

Canopy top surface, before application of coating (p. 51)

Canopy, installation of bottom-shell ferro-cement panels (p. 52)

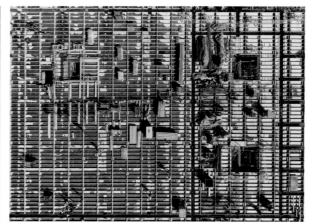

Canopy, installation of bottom-shell ferro-cement panels (p. 53)

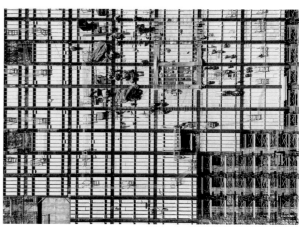

Canopy, installation of bottom-shell ferro-cement panels (pp. 55–57)

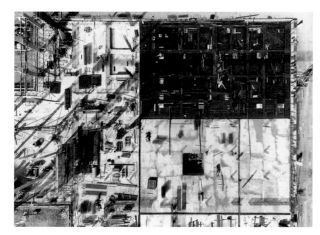

Library, ground-level slab (p. 59)

Library "Book Castle" concrete structure (pp. 61–63)

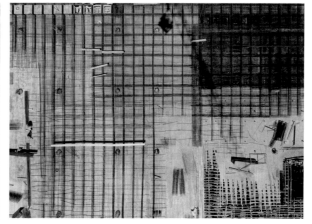

Library, reinforcement to roof slab (p. 65)

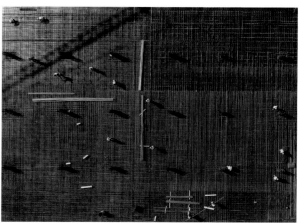

Car Park, typical floor reinforcement (p. 67)

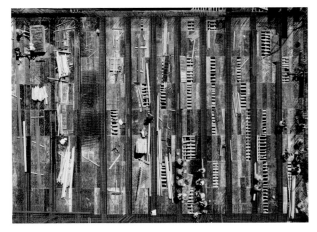

Opera, reinforcement to roof slab (p. 69)

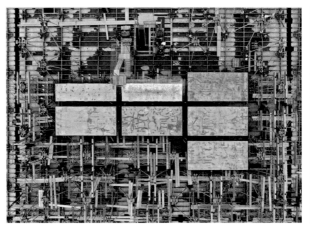

Ferro-cement panels ready for placement (p. 70)

Canopy, installation of top-shell ferro-cement panels (p. 71)

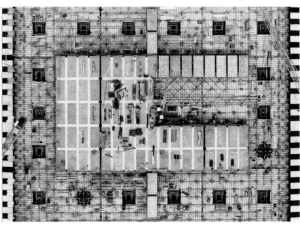

Canopy, installation of top-shell ferro-cement panels, central zone (p. 73)

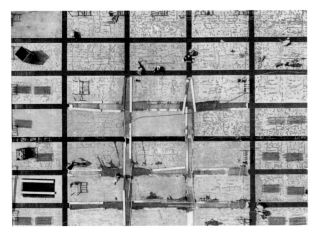

Canopy top shell, reinforcement to splice zones (p. 75)

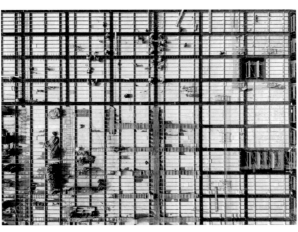

Canopy bottom shell, reinforcement to splice zones (p. 77)

Car Park, typical floor slab (p. 79)

Hill park, north entry, east (p. 80)

Canal building, ferro-cement roof (p. 81)

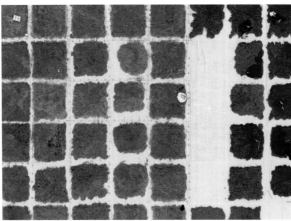

Library green roof, placement of topsoil (p. 83)

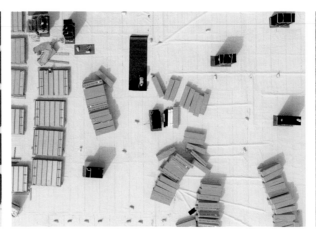

Library, roof insulation (p. 84)

Library green roof, placement of topsoil (p. 85)

Steel spider brackets for Canopy, temporary storage on ground (p. 86)

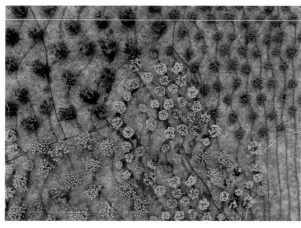

Planting shrubs on the Hill (p. 87)

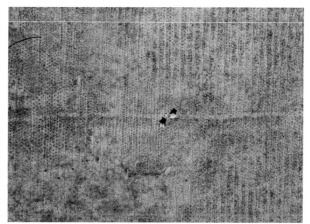

Library roof, planting plug plants (p. 89)

Canopy top surface, installation of couplers for photovoltaic panels (p. 91)

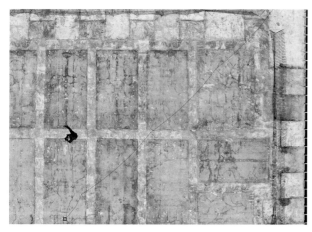

Canopy top surface, preparation for painting (p. 93)

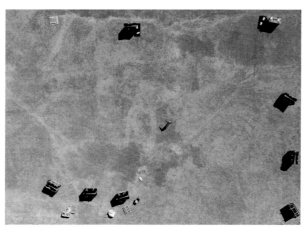

Library green roof, preparation for planting (p. 94)

Canopy top surface, before application of coating (p. 95)

Mediterranean Gardens on the Hill (p. 96)

Opera, ground-level slab, seismic isolator bottom plates (p. 97)

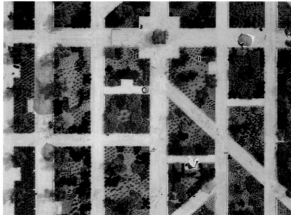

Mediterranean Gardens on the Hill (p. 99)

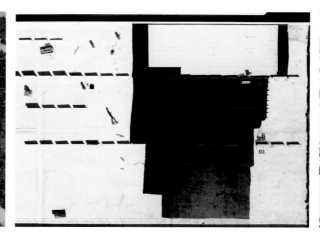

Car Park, roof waterproofing (pp. 101–3)

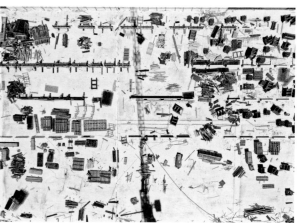

Car Park, hardscaping the roof (pp. 105–7)

Canopy, central-zone scaffolding (p. 108)

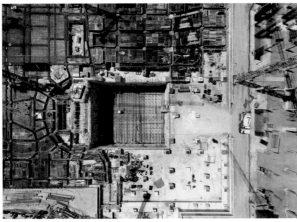

Opera, reinforcement to stage pit and ground-level slab (p. 109)

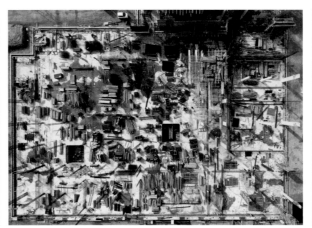

Library, ground-level slab (p. 111)

Library and Car Park, ground-level slabs separated by the "Canyon" (service road) (pp. 113–15)

Canopy top surface, applying protective coating (p. 117)

Canopy top surface, applying protective coating (p. 118)

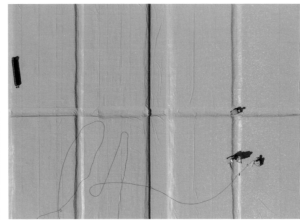

Canal, waterproofing membrane (p. 119)

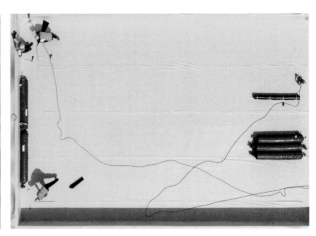

Canal, waterproofing membrane (p. 120)

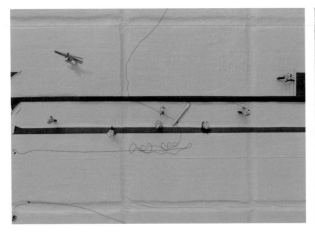

Canal, waterproofing membrane (p. 121)

Canopy, installation of bottom-shell ferro-cement panels (p. 123)

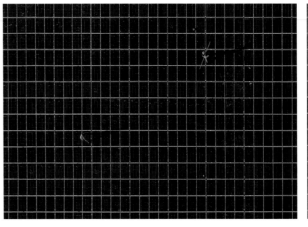

Photovoltaic panels on top of Canopy (p. 124)

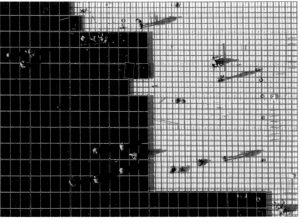

Canopy, metal supporting grid for photovoltaic panels (p. 125)

154

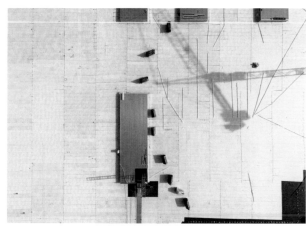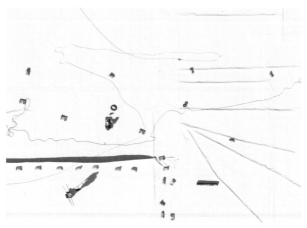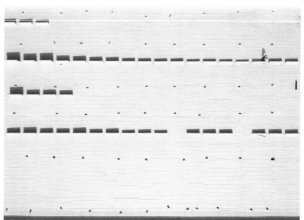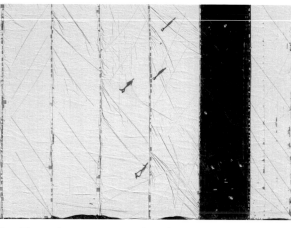

Library skylights, roof, preparation for waterproofing (p. 127)   Library roof, preparation for waterproofing (p. 129)   Car Park, hardscaping the roof (p. 131)   Great Lawn, temporary protection of the soil (p. 133)

Acknowledgments

The publication of a book is often compared to a long-distance race. It requires systematic preparation, a steady pace through all the stages of its long course, and endurance for the difficult last mile. But in contrast to the loneliness felt by a distance runner, I had the fortune to have many valuable companions by my side during the course of this marathon.

The paternity of the ideas—both of photographing the construction of the Stavros Niarchos Foundation Cultural Center and the creation of this publication—belongs to Yerassimos Yannopoulos, advisor to the Foundation. He not only inspired the present book, but as a loving parent also followed its development stage by stage, assisting at points when the pace slowed and offering solutions whenever they were needed. I express my gratitude to him, hoping that the results justify his continuous support.

None of the photographs of the book could have been taken without the help of Ilias Soumpasis, aerial operator of the tower cranes at the SNFCC work site, who took care of my repeated ascents and—more importantly—safe descents from the great height that the aerial photography required. Hanging from a metal basket, I encountered an unknown world. Ilias familiarized me with that world and with the many demands of visiting it; I thank him for arranging everything so that I might devote myself without distraction to the view I had before my lens. Warm gratitude is due also to Michalis Papafilippou, project manager of the work site, for putting the cranes at my disposal despite their heavy workload, and for all his assistance in the photographic documentation of the project. I thank all the workers of the consortium Salini Impregilo–Terna for their cooperation over the course of nearly a decade, in particular the crane operators, in whose hands I entrusted my life at each ascent over the work site.

During the gradual materialization of this publication, I had the fortune to have by my side Akis Ioannides, architect, graphic designer, and the best colleague imaginable, and Annie Ragia, director of the Melissa Publishing House. Akis undertook the design of this book and edited each part of it as a director would a cinematic work: he was aware of the smallest detail, provided solutions, and politely intervened whenever I was in danger of straying from the goal. Annie embraced the idea of this publication from the beginning and, drawing on her great experience, gathered and coordinated the group that brought the effort to a happy conclusion. She invited the collaboration of Christopher Hudson, Publisher, The Museum of Modern Art in New York, who served as an advisor on the present volume, and of Sarah Meister, curator in MoMA's Department of Photography, who edited and sequenced the photographic narrative of the book. I am deeply grateful for their guidance.

At Yale University Press, I offer my thanks to John Donatich, Director of Publications, Patricia Fidler, Publisher of Art and Architecture books, and Katherine Boller, Editor of Art and Architecture books; their support of this publication ensures its international presence.

The present volume would be lacking without the written contributions of the distinguished architect of the project, Renzo Piano, and of Katharine Storr and Robert Storr, architect and former Dean of the School of Art at Yale University, respectively. To Piano I offer my heartfelt thanks, in the hope that the published photographs may illuminate an unexpected side of the successive actualization of his architecture. Katharine and Robert Storr's thoughtful essay offered me new insights into my own photographs. I am honored to have their words in this publication.

Invaluable to the completion of the publication was the contribution of Nikos Markou, colleague and friend, who processed the digital files with professionalism and skill, ensuring the quality of the photographs. I also thank Freya Evenson and Thetis Xanthaki for their excellent translations of the texts into English and Greek, respectively, and Diana Stoll and Ourania Iordanidou for the care and attention with which they edited them.

Finally, I wish to express my deepest gratitude to the Stavros Niarchos Foundation for the best collaboration I have had the fortune to experience in my professional career. Through all these years, at every level of interaction with the Foundation, I encountered only people who offered me kind words, recognition for my work, and the creative freedom to improve the photographic results each time. Especially warm thanks are due to Andreas Dracopoulos, Co-President of the Board of Directors of the Stavros Niarchos Foundation, for supporting the effort from beginning to end. I am grateful also to the team at the Foundation with which I worked during the many years of this effort: to Giorgos Agouridis, member of the Board of Directors of the Cultural Center, for his administrative attention and organization of the course of the publication; to Stelios Vasilakis, Director of Programs and Strategic Initiatives, who, with his extensive experience in the publishing field, generously conferred with Yale University Press; to Theodore Maravelias, architect and Chief Technical Officer, and Vagelis Alysandratos, Project Director of Construction Delivery at Faithful & Gould, for contributing the explanatory texts for the images and enriching them with necessary technical information; to Lenia Vlavianou, Assistant Chief Operating Officer and Director of Public Affairs, for her discreet and always timely support; and of course to the entire communications team at the Foundation, who greatly contributed to the successful completion of this publication. It would be no exaggeration to note that the volume in hand belongs as much to Asimina Koutroumpousi—architect and Technical Officer—as it does to me. If every aspect of the project was documented sufficiently and on time, it is due to her efforts, as she was responsible all these years for the cooperation and communication between the Foundation and the author. I thank her for all she has done for me.

This book would have remained in the realm of thought and desire, without ever being materialized, if Erato Koutsoudaki, my wife and companion, had not been here with me. Without her support, tolerance, endurance, and discussions, this enterprise would never have moved beyond words to become action.

This publication is dedicated to my two girls, Erato and Dido, who give meaning to this life.

Y. Y.

Tracing the master plan onsite

Contributors

Renzo Piano (b. 1937) studied architecture in Florence and Milan, graduating from the Politecnico di Milano in 1964. In 1971, Piano and Richard Rogers established the Piano & Rogers architectural firm in London; together they were awarded the commission to design the Centre Georges Pompidou in Paris. In the early 1970s, Piano began a long collaboration with engineer Peter Rice, forming the Atelier Piano & Rice, which operated from 1977 to 1981.

The Renzo Piano Building Workshop was established in 1981; today it has a staff of 150 and offices in Paris, Genoa, and New York. The workshop has designed buildings all around the world, including, among many others: the Menil Collection, Houston; the Fondation Beyeler Museum, Basel; London Bridge Tower (the Shard), London; and the New York Times headquarters, New York.

Among the accolades for Piano's achievements are the RIBA Royal Gold Medal for Architecture (1989), the Praemium Imperiale in Tokyo (1995), the Pritzker Architecture Prize (1998), and the Gold Medal from the American Institute of Architects (2008). Along with the Stavros Niarchos Foundation Cultural Center, Piano's most recent projects include the Torre Intesa Sanpaolo, Turin, and the new Whitney Museum of American Art, New York.

Katharine Storr (b. 1986) earned her Master's degree at the Yale School of Architecture, where an interest in art led her to participate in several projects exploring the intersection of art with architecture. This included XS, an interdisciplinary art collaborative that held pop-up exhibitions around New Haven, Connecticut, as well as contributing research for the book *Exhibiting Architecture: A Paradox?* (2015). While studying for her Bachelor's degree in mathematics at Haverford College, she interned at the Peggy Guggenheim Collection in Venice. Ms. Storr has also had a lifelong interest in theater, and before pursuing architecture professionally she worked in a Broadway costume department. She currently works at Foster + Partners in London and is on the board of the American Institute of Architects UK.

Robert Storr (b. 1949) is a professor of painting / printmaking and the former Dean of the School of Art at Yale University. He was Curator and then Senior Curator in the Department of Painting and Sculpture at The Museum of Modern Art, New York, from 1990 to 2002. In 2002 he was named the first Rosalie Solow Professor of Modern Art at New York University's Institute of Fine Arts, a position he held until 2006. He was the Director of the 2007 Venice Biennale, the first American-born curator to be named to that post, and from 2005 to 2011 he was Consulting Curator of Modern and Contemporary Art at the Philadelphia Museum of Art. He has been a contributing editor at *Art in America* since 1981 and writes frequently for *Artforum*, *Parkett*, *Art Press* (Paris), *Frieze* (London), and *Corriere della Sera* (Milan). He has written numerous catalogs, articles, and books, including *Philip Guston* (1986), *Cage: 6 Paintings by Gerhard Richter* (2009), *"September": A History Painting by Gerhard Richter* (2010), and the forthcoming *Intimate Geometries: The Work and Life of Louise Bourgeois*.

Yiorgis Yerolymbos (b. 1973) studied photography in Athens and architecture in Thessaloniki. He earned a graduate degree in Image and Communication (1998) at Goldsmith's College, University of London, and produced a doctoral dissertation in Art and Design (2007) at the University of Derby (U.K.). He taught photography at the School of Architecture, University of Thessaly, from 2008 to 2011.

Yerolymbos's photographic work has been featured in solo and group exhibitions in Greece and abroad, and has been published in many art and architecture books. He chooses to photograph "humanized" landscapes, with a focus on the interface of nature and human intervention as manifested in the contemporary landscape. In particular, he photographs "intermediate" landscapes—sections of the environment that are in transition due to human activity. In 2008, with the support of a Fulbright scholarship, Yerolymbos traveled across the United States from East to West and back, photographing the American landscape. He has participated in the Venice Biennale of Architecture twice: in 2012, with large-scale works on the city of Athens, and again in 2014, with landscape images of Greece. In 2013 his photographs were included in *Everywhere but Now*, the main exhibition of the 4th Biennale of Contemporary Art of Thessaloniki, curated by Adelina von Fürstenberg.

Since 2007, Yerolymbos has been the official photographer of the construction of the Stavros Niarchos Foundation Cultural Center.

View from crane due northeast

Produced by MELISSA Publishing House LLC

General Coordination
Annie Ragia

Publication Consultant
Christopher Hudson, Publisher, The Museum of Modern Art, New York

Design
Akis Ioannides

Photography
Sarah Meister, Curator, Department of Photography, The Museum of Modern Art, New York: Editor
Nikos Markou: Processing

Editorial
Theodore Maravelias, architect, and Vagelis Alysandratos, civil/structural engineer: Timeline and Plate texts
Diana C. Stoll: Editing of English texts
Ourania Iordanidou: Editing of Greek texts
Freya Evenson: Translation from Greek to English
Thetis Xanthaki: Translation from English to Greek

Printing and binding
Trifolio, Verona, Italy

Yale University Press
John Donatich, Director
Patricia Fidler, Publisher, Art & Architecture
Katherine Boller, Editor, Art & Architecture

Library of Congress Control Number: 2016949290

ISBN 978-0-300-22681-2

Distributed by
Yale University Press
302 Temple Street
P.O. Box 209040
New Haven, CT 06520-9040
yalebooks.com/art

Printed in Italy
10 9 8 7 6 5 4 3 2 1